ABOUT THE

The Reverend Jonathan Tapsell is . _ _ ---,
author/filmmaker who founded the world's largest occult festival,
Occulture, in Brighton. He celebrates his birthday on July 22nd, the
Feast Day of Mary Magdalene (who some Catholics claim was a
demon-possessed prostitute). The church that ordained him once
gave refuge to draft dodgers during the Vietnam War; the ethos of
his ministry is to provide shelter from society to the outsider.

The Reverend Tapsell has archived the world's largest
collection of Wiccan materials, bequeathed by the late Doreen
Valiente, often called the Mother of Modern Witchcraft. He is
currently working on books about occult conspiracies and the
hidden mystical sites of London.

# PORN=AGAIN CHRISTIAN

## Rev. Jonathan Tapsell

### One Englishman's Startling Adventures in the UK Sex Trade!

Pennant Books

First published in paperback 2009
by Pennant Books

Text copyright © Jonathan Tapsell 2008

The moral right of the author has been asserted.

Pennant Books' True Crime  Series is edited by Paul Woods.

British Library Cataloguing-in-Publication Data:
A catalogue record for this book is available on request from
The British Library

ISBN 978-1-906015-33-6

Design & Typeset by Envy Design Ltd

Printed and bound in Turkey by Mega Printing

Pennant Books
A division of Pennant Publishing Ltd
PO Box 5675
London W1A 3FB

www.pennantbooks.com

# CONTENTS

# INTRODUCTION

I met the author of this delightful and amusing book in 2001, when I went to Brighton to give a talk at the Occulture festival, founded by Jonathan Tapsell. The friend who was responsible for introducing us was a brilliant and highly literate Irishman named Gabriel Duffy, who shares with Jonathan a Rabelaisian sense of humour and a casual, highly readable style.

Sadly, Gabriel died last December by falling off a wagon – not literally, but symbolically, for he shared with many of his fellow countrymen a tendency to try and counterbalance bursts of overindulgence with determined teetotalism. The sexual frankness of his autobiography, *Sham to Rock* (2003), like his frankness about his alcoholism, caused dismay to his relatives and outrage to many reviewers.

Now, although I live in Cornwall, I had been familiar with the South Coast for many years, for a friend named Stuart Holroyd ran a school for foreign students in Hove, and I often drove down there to lecture. Stuart, as with myself, had been labelled an 'Angry Young Man' in the 1950s and, now that rather vertiginous period was over, faced the problem of making a living, like the rest of us. His home was half-school, half-hotel. And it was there, in the 60s, that I learned that there was a great deal of witchcraft around the area, and that signs of Pagan ceremonies could often be observed in the woods.

Such things continue to make good copy for journalists. Jonathan Tapsell was working as a documentary filmmaker when a friend of his, Derek Leon Taylor, died in rather puzzling circumstances. The press began to report rumours that he had been a black magician, and had got what was coming to him. Since Jonathan knew Taylor as a generous, kindly man, he did his best to correct these reports. And it was when he realised that no one was interested in his corrections that he conceived the idea of launching an 'Occulture' festival in Brighton, and inviting some of the so-called black magicians and witches to come and explain their beliefs.

Since my 700-page work *The Occult* (1971) was one of the most widely-read volumes on the subject at the time, it was inevitable that I should be invited to speak. Always glad of an opportunity of spending an evening with Gabriel, I was a regular guest at the festival until the last one in 2003.

In effect, Jonathan found himself in the same position I was in before I published *The Outsider* in 1956, and was rocketed to notoriety among such writers as John Osborne, John Braine, Arnold Wesker and Alan Sillitoe. Controversy and independence had developed in Jonathan a taste for freedom. I had slept out on Hampstead Heath to save rent money. Jonathan tried working in an office but he felt stifled, and soon felt the need to move on.

What happened then is chronicled in this book. It was a typical odyssey in search of independence, of a kind of which dozens, if not hundreds, of parallels could be offered from the past half-century. He became manager of a fish and chip shop just before it opened on New Year's Eve; then, having brought this project to success, he again felt the need to move on. Since he was an experienced photographer and documentary filmmaker, he became the manager of a small agency for female models, including a pretty blonde who became his girlfriend.

There is an uproarious sketch in Chapter Two of a dubious character known as 'Steve the Spank', because of his involvement with corporal punishment; unfortunately, Steve's visit to Brighton to publicly photograph girls' bottoms encased in school knickers leads to an uncomfortable interview with the police. Steve proves to be a conman, and this section ends with the delightful comment: 'One of the most surprising things I learned about Steve during my time with him was that, despite his hedonistic lifestyle, he was a deeply religious man. I can only wonder what he would have been like if he was godless.'

Later, in his capacity as cameraman, Jonathan films a black lady dominatrix and two of her pathetic clients who pay to be dominated – which includes sticking out their tongues to allow her to stub out lighted cigarettes on them, and drinking her urine. This is followed by what is, for me, one of the oddest and most fascinating episodes in the book: how, on his way home, he experiences a 'dreamlike message . . . from nowhere' that 'left me wondering whether I was actually drawing certain forces towards me, like a magnet . . .' Passing a mound surrounded by railings, 'I stepped into a self-contained bubble of space and time.' An insistent voice in his head begins repeating the word 'Babalon', which means the gateway to the goddess. Two years later, he discovers that the mound – which holds Penton Reservoir – once contained a stone circle and was a druidic ritual site.

My own suspicion is that something deep inside him rebelled at the SM filming session and responded thankfully to the ritual associations of the druidic mound, like a drowning man gulping deep breaths of air. Jung said the soul has a religious function, and I suspect this is what stirred into life as he passed the reservoir.

I am reminded of something that happened to the drama critic Kenneth Tynan, a devotee of flagellation, after a game-playing SM session with two women. Tynan admitted to being deeply ashamed of these charades, in some of which he dressed as a woman, and wondered if he was not also attracting some sinister forces like a magnet. He described a 'literally diabolic dream' at St Tropez, about a masochistic girl in a cellar, naked, covered with excrement, her hair shaved off and dozens of drawing pins driven into her head. 'At this point I wake up filled with horror. And at once, dogs in the hotel grounds began to bark pointlessly, as they are said to when the King of Evil, invisible to men, passes by. I really felt as if my mind had been the temporary harbour of an evil spirit, sent to deliver an obscure and obscene warning.'

Is this the basic meaning of Jonathan's dreamlike experience? The more I think of it, the more likely it seems. It certainly illuminates for me my own response to the book. Jonathan had decided to present the Occulture festivals because he felt there was something important in the Pagan cultural revolt they represented. Yet a part of him clung to a Christian moral heritage. When I asked him about his 'reverend' title, he replied, 'I am a Christian reverend of the Universal Church of the USA – the church that gave the title to draft dodgers to avoid Vietnam. I liked that idea and asked them to ordain me in 2001, which they did.' And now he tells me he is planning another Occulture festival, which seems to be yet another response to the 'inner signal' experienced in Pentonville Road.

When I was in Paris at the age of 19, I became involved with a group of expatriate writers who produced pornography for Olympia Press, run by Maurice Girodias, one of whose projects was to publish English versions of the novels of the Marquis de Sade. The brilliant Alexander Trocchi, who was one of the leading lights of this circle, even organised sex sessions that included flogging. But although I had no moral objection to supporting oneself with porn, I never quite came to terms with it, harbouring a sneaking feeling that you cannot play with tar without getting your hands dirty. And this, I suspect, describes the Reverend Jonathan's attitude towards it.

The truth is that pornography is a question that no serious writer can ignore. In the Victorian age, no one had any doubt that it was, quite simply, a manifestation of moral evil, and writers like Ibsen, Shaw, Wells and Lawrence did their best to create a more tolerant attitude to it. The verdict of the *Lady Chatterley's Lover* trial in 1960 demonstrated their victory. Yet when I read of Tynan's flogging sessions, and Jonathan's afternoon with the black goddess Sardar, I have to admit that my own attitude is still ambivalent.

What repels me about porn? The Moors Murderer, Ian Brady, put his finger on the problem when he admitted that, after several sex murders, 'I felt old at 26. Everything was ashes. I felt there was nothing of interest – nothing to hook myself on to. I had experienced everything.'

I began to observe the same during a period when I was studying Sade. I felt he was suffering from some mental illness that separated him from reality. He obviously believed that committing sadistic rape would connect him to reality. Instead, it brought the feeling Brady calls 'ashes', that nothing is real.

What is missing in such a state of mind is an element for which I once coined the phrase 'the vibration of seriousness'. Gurdjieff said we are all asleep 99 percent of the time, but when we experience the vibration of seriousness it is as if we begin to awake.

Pornography is based on the fact that sexual excitement also has the effect of waking us up. And we falsely assume that if we could carry this to some kind of extreme, it would have the effect of jarring us into permanent wide-awakeness. This is an error, like that of a concentration camp victim who believes that, if only he were free, he would eat and eat and eat until he felt fully alive – when in fact it would only make him feel sick.

That is why Jonathan's Pentonville Road experience 'pertains to the thread of this book'.

When I suggested I should write this, Jonathan was dubious, obviously feeling that the book should not be taken too seriously. But after reading it through in a single sitting (and once again before writing), I was more than happy to provide an introduction. For I believe he has written a more important book than he realises.

COLIN WILSON, February 2009

## CHAPTER 1

# FIRST ENTRY – THE VIRGINAL AWAKENING

### The Pen is Mightier than the Film Camera?

Essentially, I am a documentary filmmaker. People and lifestyles fascinate me. Writing is my second string when I have a story to tell. An old friend of mine once said, 'The first law of man is: Never put anything in writing.' He is probably right, but I could not leave this story unwritten any longer. Film was not the right medium for this tale, albeit my natural reflex.

This particular book is about the porn industry and its close cousin prostitution. Having said that, it is not a work of objective journalism, like, say, an embedded journalist covering a war; this is the soldier-of-fortune's story. I wanted to be in close to my subjects – a sort of gonzo journalism, where the writer is as much the story as the subject. When I came across the right conditions, the story unfolded with wild abandon, the subjects proving as addictive as the lifestyle. It was like coming up on a crazy drug. 21st century pornographers are outlaws, living as they do on the outside of society. As I began writing this tale, I found myself alongside them, separated from the herd, and so for a short while I too lived completely outside of society and its control. But let me begin at the beginning.

I started working in the film business in the early 1990s, quite by accident, while out in Malaysia. It was my pen that got me the job as I was good at composing storylines and scripts. Here we were, making action movies on a shoestring budget with all hands to the pump. There were no real pyrotechnics involved, so we taught ourselves how to blow up roughly constructed bridges with dynamite. When we got it wrong we nearly got killed, so we learned fast. Bullets and guns were real, with permits for guns issued by the local police, and to carry a gun without the permit carried the death penalty.

Professional actors were few and far between, so the director, Toby Russell, trawled the toughest ghettos in Asia to recruit martial artists more given to street fighting than anything else. The exception was the Taiwanese star Robert Tai, who was so fast that, when he kicked four men, touching each one fleetingly, you could not really detect it with the naked eye. He was a blur, and the film editor actually had to slow the film down to catch his kicks.

Toby Russell was a driven man, and he feared only one thing in this world – failure. He spoke fluent Hokkien and Mandarin

# FIRST ENTRY – THE VIRGINAL AWAKENING

Chinese and was well versed in the ways of the Orient. Standing a mighty six feet six inches, although not an expert martial artist himself, he was certainly something of a hard man who could take care of himself with street-fighting techniques. Toby worked 20 hours round the clock in the jungle, harassed by flies, spiders, snakes, monsoon rains, government censors who interfered with the scripts, red tape and more, but he never once complained. He lived and breathed the film and everyone respected him. He was inspiring to work alongside.

On the last big film, Toby had managed to secure the services of two tough-looking Hollywood cameramen who had worked with legendary film director Sam Peckinpah, the father of slow-motion photography. When Toby asked one of the cameramen if Sam Peckinpah was an exciting character to work with, he replied, 'No more than you are, son, no more than you.'

It was a touching thing to say but, looking back, very true. Toby's work paid off and he broke all Malaysian box-office receipts for his often bloodthirsty, violent action movies. Malaysian film censors must have hated him. How he made such quality 35mm films on those pitiful budgets still seem miraculous to me to this day. But I learned a lot from his attitude towards his crew, who were his extended family of outsiders. This was not work for the nine-to-five man. If you lived and breathed your work, you got results.

Back in England, I attended the Panico film school, started by Monty Python, Beatle George Harrison and some other UK film enthusiasts. Panico's remit was to nurture new film talent, and I think it has certainly done so.

Even then people often noted my aptitude to come up with plots at a moment's notice, and it seemed that my ability lay with the pen as much as with the camera. My student film was a five-minute comedy called *The Harmonica Player* filmed on 35mm, in chronological order. I was always a great one for keeping things simple. Most directors film the end, then scene 23, then scene six and then the beginning, etc. But why do it for a film short? Perhaps this is the writer in me coming out, as opposed to the director. The comedy rushes were screened at a cinema near Centrepoint, London, to a small audience of fellow film students and some of the Panico people, and my first film comedy was very well received.

Some years later, I set up a video company making short TV promos and corporate videos, and selected the cast for at least one ITN special.

When I look back, I cannot say I have led a particularly happy, successful, harmonious, contented or fruitful life, but I have managed instead to kindle a flame. Much of my life has involved tangled internal considerations of how to apply myself differently, be a unique individual and maintain some set of life principles at the same time. Perhaps this is one of the salient reasons I accepted the title Reverend from the Universal Life Church, to promote liberty and freedom in all senses.

Don't imagine for one minute that the 'Reverend' is going up into the pulpit here. I am talking about living life from opposite sides, one is the steady laborious flow of work, duty, family history and what society demands of you as an individual; the other pole is what did you do for yourself, and to what end.

This intense burning inside, caused by the search for new experiences, has caused me suffering, anguish and to commit appalling mistakes only a fool with a capital F could make. My forays into writing helped me to understand all of this, and put it into perspective, which was something videos and films could never do.

## Occulture – Brandy of the Damned?

One of the good things in my life was an odyssey of self-discovery for me. It came out of a mixture of disgust, righteous anger, a sense of injustice and the good old British sense of fair play – the result, weirdly enough, was the Occulture festival.

Having completed a documentary called *The Hex Files* with another filmmaker (which we made to sell on to terrestrial television outlets), I thanked a number of contributors for their time. One of the people key to the research and also post-production was a man called Derek Leo Taylor, who was a very eccentric healer, herbalist, astronomer, psychic and Pagan, but above all else a gentleman of the old school. He deserved all credit for his generosity, time and support throughout the production.

When he died on a beach in Rustington, West Sussex, under mysterious circumstances, the press went for him. For the next few days, various local newspapers repeated hearsay, rumour and innuendo about Taylor. These spurious articles fed the line that Taylor was a black magician involved in some dark, unholy act before he died. It was a media circus and not at all respectful to surviving relatives or to such a good man, in my opinion. When I tried to contact the editor of the *Evening Argus*, Sussex's biggest newspaper, in order to straighten things out, the response was disappointing. I wanted to calm things down but I was rebuffed with a short email. Naturally, I thought it was poorly handled, chiefly because I felt the truth about the man's life had been ignored in favour of lurid headlines. Everyone in the media business advised me to stay away, telling me it was useless to complain and that it was standard practice to class people with Pagan beliefs as black magicians and make them out to be evil. In other words, I was being a bit naive not to accept that point of view. I felt a sense of outrage as Derek had been such a kind person in life, often helping those less fortunate and always very charitable to the sick. When I was informed that another alternative group of people had been subjected to similar treatment because they had chosen to adorn a mountain retreat with art, I was confused. Did other writers really behave in this way? Could *anyone* be vilified, attacked, for no good reason? When I was told that simply not being Christian or accepting any belief outside of the 'big five' – Hinduism, Islam, Buddhism, Judaism and Christianity – was risky, I was appalled. Atheism was safe, I was informed by one veteran journalist, because a person did not really believe anything. This was the state of play in the year 2000 AD.

## FIRST ENTRY – THE VIRGINAL AWAKENING

It was then, in a fit of pique, that I decided to invite all of those who had been attacked in the media for their spiritual beliefs to a conference of heretics. To provoke things further, I called it Occulture (occult = hidden, culture = lifestyle). Anyone who had been victimised, portrayed as evil, such as witches etc, was invited to speak about it. Naturally, I informed the press, who sensed they should ignore it, probably because they were incapable of understanding what it was all about. We were biting back.

So began the first Occulture festival with an air of vitriol.

The guests were Emrys the Shaman, who had been stitched up by the tabloids for 'gun running': read charity work; journalist, writer and UK emissary of the Church of Satan, the Irreverend Gavin Baddeley, who came for the fun as much as anything else; another writer, Jeff Merrifield, talked about the Damanhur Community of Italy, which had been stormed by the military. Lastly, to try to give a new explanation of Paganism, there was Ralph Harvey. Ralph was definitely one of the best public speakers who ever graced the Occulture festival stage. It was said he was a witch who presided over 200 covens in West Sussex alone – we were not laying things on lightly at the festival!

A couple of organisations withdrew before the grand opening, but the festival's first night attracted a full house of about 60 people. Over six weeks there were four talks. These first brave contributors spoke to small but attentive audiences, and guests became really passionate about it all. It had been a success, but that was that.

However, it didn't end there, as David Bramwell of *Cheeky Brighton Guide* urged that another festival should follow in 2001. He was a good persuader and I am grateful for that.

The following year, by popular demand, the Occulture festival had grown, and more people wanted to speak out about their hidden beliefs, on what they described as a positive platform. The most moving of these, in my opinion, was a live link-up with elderly Pagan Eleanor Bone. The spritely 89-year-old spoke about her beliefs; she was initiated into the secrets of these country ways in 1941, when it was still a criminal offence to be a witch. During 1942, another woman was jailed for two years for such offences. Eleanor called for a tolerance of all religions and respect for the wisdom of the ages. The audience erupted when she finished her speech and she received a standing ovation. At the same festival, philosophers such as Colin Wilson, author of *The Outsider*, stood alongside witches calling for tolerance. It was a watershed and totally took me by surprise.

In 2002, the Occulture festival doubled in size once more, this time attracting audiences of up to 250 people at a time. This festival was opened by the Mayor of Brighton, who also saw that there was a need to end the spurious attacks by the press on people's faiths. Our festival remit was simple: no sexism, no racism, no violence and definitely no preaching. People just came to express something spiritual, whether it was in word, film, sculpture, art, music, dance or mime. The Tibetan government stated their case for liberation and peace, while on other stages Chaos magicians, tarot readers, psychics and filmmakers all called for an end to persecution. It was a bit freaky for me when I received word that the Dalai Lama approved of the Occulture festivals. He reportedly wished there were more of such meets in the world. It seemed the event had gained considerable momentum. It really had become a festival of people fed up with press vilification, looking for a new vision.

I did have one little issue of in-house politics to deal with, when a Pagan asked me indignantly why I had chosen a saxophone-playing transvestite to compere the event, accusing him of bringing the whole thing into disrepute.

My reply was even and cool: 'You are the man who wears an iron mask in the woods, with horns on it, surrounded by naked women worshipping fertility gods. Do you really consider yourself or anyone else here *normal* in the eyes of society?'

He and his wife laughed jovially and graciously conceded my point.

I always defended my guests to the hilt, regardless of their path or personal persuasion. The press felt that too and gave me a wide berth. A run-in with the local Evangelists made me a media tiger and I always thank them for the opportunity to stand up for the oppressed, as it did everyone a lot of good.

The Evangelical Christians absolutely hated Occulture and all it stood for. After one such festival, they dared to suggest that we had sacrificed animals on stage. It was a crass, stupid lie; Pagans are some of the most nature-loving people around. But, over the years, certain Evangelists had become accustomed to getting away with these sorts of ridiculous allegations. Some unscrupulous journalists and editors had published these types of stories, and it was precisely why Occulture had come into existence in the first place. I for one did not appreciate being lied about in the newspapers. Occulture sprang into action, and we answered the spurious allegation with such passion that, it encouraged literally hundreds of Brighton people to support a festival aimed at giving people free expression. In fact, the broadside that I submitted to the papers did not hold back, and had to be toned down before publication. (The festival compere, John Beham-Payne, also wrote a reply.)

In short, I charged my Evangelist witch-finder with medieval-style persecution. I stated that the days when the unenlightened Christian Church attacked gays, unmarried mothers, people drinking after ten on a Sunday, interracial marriages and more were over. My accuser's hatred and bigotry had finally come home to roost. No one wanted to be seen to support such views in the 21st century. The Brighton people had warmly accepted Occulture, clearly rejecting the Evangelist claims of animal sacrifice. It had been a very stupid own goal on their part and we milked it for every drop of publicity. In effect, we played them at their own game.

An air of fear had been lifted and, for the first time ever, I saw people openly declaring that they were Pagans or Wiccans, visibly straightening up and saying things like 'I am a Pagan and also a teacher,' or 'I am a witch and I work in the local council,' or 'I am a Shamen-healer who is a delivery driver,' or whatever. These people had suddenly discovered self-respect and self-assurance, and it was good to see it. Occulture seemed to be doing a good job, having taken a stand against insidious, sniping witch-hunting, which leads to fear and persecution. By 2002, those days should have been over.

Perhaps my personal highlight was in 2003, when the festival attracted over 2000 people in one day, with stallholders, a main stage with compere, a music-meditation area, a garden with marquees, film festival and more. I really knew it had become a proper festival, as opposed to a seminar or conference, when making my way around the event, I came across a marquee. What a surprise I found inside: writer Mary Hedger and her brother dressed in bright-orange boiler suits; she was reading ritual poetry and he was playing the drums. Everyone in the marquee was spellbound – literally. I didn't even know this was supposed to be happening, and I was one of the organisers. To this day I have no idea what they were actually doing. I said to myself, 'Now this is what I call a festival!' and I stood back to enjoy whatever they were performing. Elsewhere, industrial musician Z'ev, a New Yorker, had people lying down on mats listening to percussion in the dark. They were seeing things – it was a sort of guided meditation. An occult film festival offered endless esoteric films and documentaries. There were more than 50 different events happening on the day, plus an array of stallholders and exhibitors. Channel 4 documentary maker Jon Ronson was soon on the main stage speaking, and later Killing Joke's Jaz Coleman played live. It was great that everyone was giving their all – it reminded me of the old no-holds-barred days with Toby in the jungle.

Occulture is one of the reasons I became really open minded towards other people's ways, beliefs and customs. The most moving moment of the whole festival was the last one in 2003 when Vim Van Dulleman, the Dutch international pianist and mentor of the Gurdjieff dancers, described the entire history of humanity as that of crime – wars to invade land, kill, bomb, pillage corn, rape other cultures and so on, but he said, 'Here at Occulture people have learned how to respect each other …' His words trailed off, but I suddenly woke up to the fact that all of us – visitors, speakers, stallholders, technicians – had created something sacred. We had formed an international platform, not so much for ourselves, but for the personal freedom of one another. All this had come about without the aid of the government, the Church, the police, hangers-on, the press or corporate sponsors, and by standing up for ourselves. I must admit my eyes became misty, and the hairs on my neck stood up. We had managed to create a place of tolerance in a world of intolerance. It was a truly euphoric moment. Occulture 2003 was the last festival and had ended on a high point.

That year the bottom dropped out of corporate video and my business partner and I closed the business amicably. The festival was suspended by mutual agreement and I later bought the rights to it.

## The Albanian Connection

Kemptown, east of Brighton, is by local repute filled with 'piers, queers and racketeers'. The Regency buildings are pretty much uninterrupted by modern development and the far end of Kemptown has the prestigious Sussex Square (the most salubrious part of Brighton, despite what Hove residents might say), although, of course, the notorious Whitehawk area also backs on to it. But I would say that for health, lifestyle, sea views and pubs – although maybe not clubs, as I am not gay – Kemptown is as good as it gets.

I rented a two-bedroom flat in the long, windy St Georges Road, but now I had to figure out how to pay for it. I took on an office job but the walls soon closed in. Corporate clothes were suggested but there were no corporate wages to match. I found the managers to be time-serving, smarmy and self-serving individuals, and perhaps, after the intensity of my former life, a-nine-to-five in an office was a mountain I could not climb. It was not the work so much, as the increasingly hostile power politics and the boredom of the routine which, to my mind, often became unhealthy. My head was pounding; I can only describe it as a form of work claustrophobia. I needed to find either something creative or something completely outside of the norm. Nowadays, I would recognise this feeling by saying that I needed to rejoin the 'outsiders', but at that time I was still unaware of those types of things.

I tried to work in a huge industrial plant by night on 12-hour shifts. The work was mundane but, on the whole, the people there did not talk; they seemed grey, choked of life, slow to any humour or quick-witted response. I soon realised that I had to get out, before my love of life was blunted by the mindless routine.

Then, as luck would have it, I was offered a job out of the blue, by an old contact of mine who had bought a Brighton fish and chip shop. The trouble was that he had no idea how to run it, no staff and no one to train anyone who came to work there anyway. It was only a few days to New Year's Eve and he began to panic.

The shop was opposite 23 nightclubs and near the town centre and West Street, Brighton's busiest thoroughfare at night, and he knew that to be open during the evenings and nights, particularly on New Year's Eve, was crucial for revenue.

Within a day, I had the keys to the shop and the manager's job in charge of four raw recruits, in the form of stout Albanians and two Englishmen. It seemed as though none of them had even been in a fish and chip shop, let alone cooked in one. It was mayhem – people rumbled spuds (peeled them by machine) that spilled all over the floor; a gas leak nearly killed us all; there was a massive basement in which people actually got lost; we had no working extractor fan, so that the canopy actually threw fumes back out and the staff were hanging out of open windows as fumes choked us all night long – but through some sort of divine intervention, on New Year's Eve we were open for business.

We had two English counter staff to translate 'pissheadese' into English and the Albanians to keep the spuds rumbled, bring them up and learn, when they could, how to fry the food properly. The fish and burgers were my domain, and I could do both jobs at once. It was a roaring success, with burgers, fish, chips, pickled gherkins and the like sold at traditionally extortionate Brighton prices. Champagne flowed at midnight to

# FIRST ENTRY – THE VIRGINAL AWAKENING

see in the New Year of 2004, as a drunken blonde girl of about mid-twenties took off her top, exposing her pert breasts, offering herself to anyone who wanted to take her down below to the cellars. Mistletoe in hand, someone did! I knew the fish and chip shop was going to be fun. No more offices or factories for me, thank you very much.

By April, the beginning of the warm weather and the tourist season, the fish and chip shop was up to scratch. The Albanians had learned to speak reasonable English, the cooking range had been renewed with state-of-the-art technology, the gas and extractor fan were fixed, and our suppliers were marshalled into some sort of regimented supply chain.

My work life sorted, my thoughts turned to love one day when a stunning blonde, no more than 22, came in for a cup of tea. It was a weekday, just off tourist season, and she was visiting Brighton for the day. I would describe her as a younger Paris Hilton but no dumb blonde; she was intelligent, sharp and witty, standing only five feet two inches or so. We'll call her Lexie. Within an hour, I was finishing work and I invited her for a drink. She was teetotal but seemed not quite so inhibited in other areas, telling me frankly about how she was lonely and missed having a relationship. I was double her age but took it to mean that she fancied me. Egotistical, perhaps, but, well, who dares wins. When I asked her if she would like to meet again, she said she had enjoyed my company and agreed. Within two days, she was back down, dolled up to the nines and looking mighty fine; in fact, people turned their heads, probably wondering why such a stunning young lady was walking with such an old git. We hit it off and started dating. Her eyes were light blue and always sparkled, like the Brighton summer seas. One day, I woke to find she was my lover, but I hardly knew anything about her, except that she came from Streatham, South London.

At the chip shop, I was working some crazy shifts up until 4 a.m., and sometimes I needed to return at 9 a.m. It was hard work but I enjoyed each day there. Several of my media contacts looked down on me for doing what they saw as menial work, but in fact I was probably using more brain power in cooking than in just clicking a mouse all day long. It was the first time I realised that much of the media can be a bit snobbish and overinflated, and I was glad that I was doing something earthy once again.

The Albanian workers were good lads, never leaving you short staffed or coming out with bullshit. If they were ill or hungover, I would send them downstairs to sleep it off on the chest freezers below, until I needed their help at that crucial mad rush between 2 and 3 a.m. I looked after them and they looked after me. Occasionally, on a Saturday before the rush, I would order in a load of cans of beer, and let them go off on their pressing nocturnal secret affairs. Often they got a call and rushed off somewhere, but I never made it my business to enquire too deeply into their affairs.

The Albanians were a very tight-knit community, with contacts among the Kosovans, Macedonians, Montenegrins and even

## FIRST ENTRY – THE VIRGINAL AWAKENING

Italians. I christened the shop the Albanian Embassy, as they came in for advice on tax, MOTs, mobile phones, housing benefit and work. I dispensed my wisdom generously and made friends with a large number of them. I liked the Albanians as they were hard working, good humoured, well mannered and always down-to-earth. Eventually, there were so many of them coming in that we had a coffee machine installed to serve them their favourite espresso. They often joked that because of my facial features, short black hair and build I looked Albanian. I even used to play along and wind up newcomers from Albania who didn't know me, telling them that I was originally from Cucksi, a village in Northern Albania. As often as not they would reply in Albanian, thinking I was the real McCoy. Slowly I began to pick up a few words, starting, as you do, with swear words.

Near to the fish and chip shop was a 24-hour café called Buddies. It was the haunt of mom and pop by day, very touristy, all fish and chips, pasta and pizzas, but by night it was one of the central hubs of Brighton, with a real buzz about the place. Doormen, actors, celebrities, private detectives, hookers, hen parties, clubbers, serious gangsters, taxi drivers, footballers and local faces converged on the place. It definitely had a night-time vibe and once you were known in Buddies you were known in Brighton – the *real* Brighton. This was also another central hangout for the Albanians. It was here along the seafront strip, near all the nightclubs, that little boys often became big boys, looking for a very different type of coke and some serious action. But Buddies would never tolerate drug dealing.

The Albanians I knew hated drugs but they liked coffee, red wine, lager, maybe a single scotch. I rarely saw any Albanian drunk like the English people in Brighton; they tended to be womanisers, enjoyed a moderate amount of alcohol and were fond of expensive items such as good cars, watches, clothes and accessories. One important thing to learn about Albanians is that they can take care of themselves if it comes to trouble. They seem to be scared of no one. I think they would die fighting before being intimidated and appear to have no qualms about fisticuffs or stabbings. Revenge is a big factor if you cross them.

I learned this the hard way at the fish and chip shop. A disturbance took place at 1 a.m., involving several studenty types. No big deal but a licensed security man who patrolled two or three establishments near by stepped in. He was a big lad, ex-para, ex-Met, about mid-fifties and more than capable of taking the situation in hand. He was well known in Brighton and considered one of the nicest doormen in the area. I really liked him; he was good company and always jovial. Everything seemed to be in hand, until a rather troublesome man mountain appeared on the scene. He was a student but a towering 6ft 5in or 6in and bare-chested, revealing a rippling Charles Atlas torso. He was young, maybe 21, and of Olympian athletic fitness. He was kicking off too.

'Gentlemen, we have a situation here,' I said to the Albanians, as a full coke can was tossed into the boiling-hot fryers, nearly causing an explosion and taking out the fryers behind the counter. We were all lucky that one of the staff fished it out almost immediately, or most of those in the fish shop would be looking like the Incredible Melting Man today. That was like a signal, an almost primeval 'Let's get the bastards!' No one needed any prompting and I was the first one in there, gate-posting the high counter and steaming into the four or five bodies clashing with the doorman, who was going under.

The man mountain had not yet lashed out, unlike his friends, but had jostled forwards to greet me. As this was going on, the Albanians had quickly armed themselves with kebab knives, which are in effect razor-sharp mini-swords and very dangerous indeed, and the long can openers made of solid steel that, used as weapons, are as deadly as any I can think of, breaking bones upon impact. The Albanian charge around the counter had women screaming and young stoned clubbers diving out of the way, creating a passage straight towards the huge student.

Once I saw the Albanians in full swing, I dived into the space between them and the man mountain, while the doorman was still struggling with at least three drunken students on the floor. Arms outstretched, I stopped the armed crew from storming into the shop front, but my back was turned to the man mountain. I told them to put down their weapons. Suddenly the top of my head was given the Judas punch, launching me straight into the Albanians, and we all went flying. Firstly, I lacerated the heel of my thumb on a knife held by those in front of me. My plunge forwards took the Albanians over a nearby table and chairs, but all was not in vain. As I went down I landed perfectly, as taught to me by John Hand, a self-defence expert and student of Jeff Thompson. You land like you are doing a press-up, letting one of your legs kick up vertically to meet the attacker's crotch. Unlikely, but I scored a bull's eye and the man mountain copped it in the crown jewels. Many people are surprised that, for a big man, who appears not to take care of himself, I am quite agile. But I have always been physically active, with tap dancing, fencing, karate, ju jitsu, badminton, stunts, yoga and jogging at different periods of my life, and I can get up off the floor as quickly as I go down. The student hadn't expected my sudden appearance back on my feet, still with my back to him, more or less at the spot where I went down. I launched a deadly elbow backwards that found its way right into the socket of his eye. He cried out in pain, reeling backwards as I spun round and gave him the *coup de grâce* – a rather excellent punch square on the jaw. He was leaning against the chip counter, shocked more than hurt, when four assassins wearing white coats and steel-toe-capped boots, dressed like doctors, steamed into him. Good health was the last thing on their minds. The white-coated Albanians dragged the big lad into a dark, urine-soaked alleyway where he was beaten unconscious. His friends were also seen off with black eyes, sore shins, loosened teeth and the like. I held my injury in a bloody wrap of kitchen towel, and the shop was closed while we cleared up the debris and made good.

To my shock, my mate the doorman said that we were probably guilty of committing assault, it was on camera and he was going to call the police. I for one was livid at this suggestion;

after all, we had protected him from his attackers. But the owner, who had just appeared in his car, stepped in to smooth things over by announcing the camera was broken. No tape existed. An unpleasant silence descended over the fish and chip shop.

Probably high on adrenalin or even semi-concussed from such a vicious blow to the head, I later told the Albanians that, if they couldn't take on an opponent without weapons, they should bring skirts into work. I may have been bragging a bit too. Anyone who knows me knows I am a pacifist, certainly no fighter. The Albanians were pissed off with me but more so with the security man. It all blew over in a couple of days but I had certainly earned my Albanian passport.

After that I finally entered the Albanian community, as word spread that the crazy Englishman at the Albanian Embassy (as they were all now calling it) had taken on a giant, without weapons, and had knocked him out as well. They loved the legend, and of course exaggeration usually follows such events. Many more Albanians came to me after that for help at the Embassy.

But by now I wanted out, as the fun, the buzz, the excitement had passed. It was time to play the Romany and move on once more. But I had made many good Albanian contacts, some of whom I intended to keep in touch with.

## The Shape of Things to Come

Unemployment, career uncertainty, dead-end jobs, bad prospects – call it what you will, but I had a lot on my mind.

Now it was time to reinvent myself, well away from the crazy world of nocturnal catering. Lexie was a boon. She moved into the flat, adding a woman's touch to the place and encouraging me to write my book *The Psychic Jungle*. The computer keyboard was worn down daily by the incessant tap of keys.

One day in an idle moment, I asked Lexie how she earned a living. I knew she was a part-time dancer but had never bothered to probe beyond that. She told me she was a lap dancer, and it explained why she was always rushing off for two days at a time, particularly at night when I had been working. I could see now that my own lifestyle had made it easy for her to do what she did without awkward questions.

As the days went by, she introduced me to some of the London dancers. They had a party at the flat and most crashed over, either in the spare room or on the sofa bed in the lounge below. It was around this time, through Lexie, that I first met Martina, a Polish brunette in her mid-twenties with a very clever business brain.

Over a few drinks, the girls told me about one club in Brighton that screwed about ten girls a month out of £300 each in back wages. The company claimed every month to have gone bankrupt, but they were still trading there, banking on the assumption that the girls had either gone back to Eastern Europe, South Africa or London. It seemed a really low trick, and it turned out that Lexie was also owed money by the club. When the girls mentioned the club owner's name I knew who he was, as he occasionally went to Buddies. I thought he was a bit of a chancer, and I remembered him as an unpleasant drunk who was rude to staff, loud and aggressive. I took note of what he owed and said no more.

Two days later I made my way to the club, which was close to Brighton city centre, and surprised the manager at his office, demanding an explanation. His attitude was one of complete disdain and contempt. He had obviously become used to ripping off the girls without any comeback. His brazen attitude infuriated me, and an argument ensued in which I accused him of cheating the dancers. He pressed a buzzer and within seconds an English security man appeared. He asked me to leave but I stated my case, that money was owed to my girlfriend, plus I wanted to expose what they were doing. Then another man appeared; he was a tall, strong-looking, dark-haired Albanian, possibly of Kosovan stock, who said, '*Sheep sha rap*' – which roughly translates as 'Fuck you and your family,' and is the worst thing you can say to anyone in Albanian. I wondered if he was saying it because he thought I was Albanian too.

The English guy added the charming rider, 'Why don't you fucking piss off?'

That did it for me – it was clearly time to leave. I nodded and smiled. 'Right then,' I said, before turning on my heel to leave the building. I harboured no grudges but would avoid such people in future. They were a trio of scum and you felt it when you met them. It was a bad vibe.

## *The Beginning*

The next day, the girls and I decided that I would organise their modelling work; I would deal with booking appointments and placing strategic ads, both in the press and on the internet. The girls benefited greatly from my sterling efforts and landed a major contract for bikinis. The newly acquired revenue heralded a change from their nightclub life and association with nasty people. Slowly their stories began to change from abusive conversations, rip-offs and generally debasing situations to tales of work, money, spin-offs and good feedback.

The girls themselves noticed through their increased work contacts and general awareness of the new business that the big money – or more accurately the *consistent* money – lay in fetish. The fetish world needed models, but, as it had a rather seedy reputation, models were scarce in certain genres, and could command huge fees. It was a model agent's dream. Fetish was gold dust. But the gold rush did not really begin until Martina heard the call of the wild.

Both Martina and Lexie expressed a liking for fetish assignments; they paid well and were fun. Most of the photographers or 'togs' were professional to work with. And the girls enjoyed the rubber, latex, light bondage and associated delights. Sex and porn were off the menu completely, and they saw assignments such as posing nude for elderly perverts as draining or degrading. So the fetish assignments seemed to be the way to go as the dollars rolled in for everyone.

Word spread fast and attracted newcomers galore. One such

character – who I found fascinating, although the girls did not share my interest – was mega fetish producer SJ, who came to me in search of, as he put it, 'the kind of girls you would find on a Brian Ferry album cover'. The twist was that he wanted to spank their arses.

SJ had had an interesting start in the business back in the early 1980s. He and his then wife made a home video featuring spanking. It must be remembered that this took place in the days when there were few such products around; there was no readily available internet and VHS had only just begun in earnest. His rare film, which was shrewdly advertised in the back of the tabloids, became an overnight success. Its scarcity made it even more valuable. SJ claimed that over the next few days he received literally piles of letters requesting the film, each containing £50 in cash, no mean sum in the early 1980s. Soon he and his wife had established their film brand and marketed the videos far and wide, accruing quite a nice profit in the process. His wife became the best-known spankee in the business, taking on the title of the 'Queen of Spanking', making SJ the king of that louche world by default. Here were two unique talents milking their erotic pastime for all its worth. Sadly for SJ, his wife later departed, leaving him with two kids and a host of tapes which were becoming increasingly worthless, due to the advent of the net among other factors.

For his next venture, SJ created a magazine called *Fessee*, although this went to the wall after a couple of issues. Further forays into this field also floundered, including failed brands

*Trestle, Spanking for Pleasure, Tallion* and *College Classics* among others. Eventually, SJ was rescued by an astute businessman who bought the back catalogue and put them on the net. SJ had sold them on for a fraction of their worth, in my opinion, and regrettably received nothing in royalties. It seemed he had missed a trick there.

However, all was not lost for SJ, as he became acquainted with a London businessman who made him editor of the spanking magazine *Janus*, based in Soho.

I liked SJ, who was good company, humorous, intelligent and full of tales of the old days. He had filmed inside army camps, milk dairies, churches and the like; it seemed he had no fear, and he had dedicated his working life to spanking girls' bottoms. He was a specialist, but I got the impression that he had seen his heyday maybe ten or 15 years earlier. Halcyon days they may have been to SJ, but of course the moment is always now.

I agreed to approach the girls and see what I could do, and he left me with a few sample videos of his work. However, when Martina and Lexie saw the videos they said they were too 80s, too passé in effect. Artistically, it was not what they wanted to be involved in, and when I told them SJ had been embroiled in one or two tabloid scandals, that was it. Lexie and Martina were very careful like that. A line was pencilled through SJ's name and he was firmly rejected. But not so the idea of working in the spanking field. It seemed both girls were interested in searching out other, more compatible producers, and I left them to it.

## *Cakes of Light*

Over the next few days, Lexie and Martina helped me write a list of ethical clubs hiring dancers and hostesses, and we started handling our own work. Within two weeks, we had dozens of girls using the agency for mostly dancing but also modelling work. I took a 15 per cent slice and I was earning a living out of it, although not a fortune. It was an easy business as long as you were organised and stayed on top of bookings. I soon got a name for being efficient, always delivering.

When called on to do so, I could also produce photographic portfolios, which sped things up as well as encouraging more models to get involved. Each day our little agency seemed to gain momentum. I didn't really need a website as a lot of girls in Soho would pass around my details, aided of course by Lexie and Martina. Martina was very cool, calm and collected, making good suggestions and keeping things very controlled. Our golden rule was never to deal with dodgy people like the Brighton club owner; no bull, just cash on the nail in return for what we offered. Once you were off our list, you never got back on again. This also became a major selling point for girls joining, who knew we only dealt with cash payers.

There was some disquiet in the camp as word spread about the way I had been treated by the Brighton club owner, but I brushed it aside as, to be truthful, my main concern was earning a good living, not retribution. But the girls continually mentioned the incident, particularly Lexie, partly I suppose because I had failed to collect her money, and they began to suggest that some sort of revenge should take place.

My involvement with magic never seems to leave me. The girls knew that, as well as organising the Occulture festival, I had also been asked to archive the world's largest witchcraft collection – that of English witch Doreen Valiente – which contains the secrets of Wicca. And they were aware that, although I am not an authority on the subject by any means, I am certainly knowledgeable about it, so they asked me how a rival might be brought down using magic. It was an innocent question, or so I thought. I answered them honestly, describing a certain way of using the Cakes of Light, which are made of menstrual blood, semen, dope, commingled sexual fluids and sacred oils, as well as your normal sugar, raisins and cinnamon, etc. Partly out of amusement, perhaps also to humour their growing hatred towards the club manager, I told them how to perform the curse while eating the cakes.

A recipe from hell it may have been, but I had no idea that they would actually bake some! When they did offer up the cakes, it was a moment of amusement, embarrassment and surprise in equal proportions.

I tried one myself to further compound my complicity in such matters. The menstrual blood made them very chewy, and I felt sick eating them, concerned that I might be risking AIDS or HIV by doing so, but soon I was on a swollen lunar high of dope and blood. The moon entered me, and we realised that it was a waning moon, when it is but a sharp sickle and perfect for black magic.

What had I done? I was not paranoid but had definitely felt

the copper-bottomed curse come to life. I immediately wanted to come down and sought refuge at the local off-licence in the form of red wine.

The girls were laughing manically by the time I came back. There was a very sinister female vibe that I cannot explain fully, but there was definitely no mercy or compassion about it; sex and death were riding about together.

With the wine I came down a bit and started to relax – this would turn out to be another big mistake.

A week or so later, on the Pagan May Day fertility festival of Beltane, I read a report that an Albanian doorman had been stabbed to death in a nearby square in Brighton. He had been knifed several times in his car after leaving the lap-dancing club where he was working at the time. Through further reports, I came to realise that it was one of the men I had argued with in the club. My Albanian contacts told me he had been killed according to the Albanian country lore of *kanun* (an honour killing similar to Italian vendetta), making the killing all the more ritualistic. The defence claimed that the murder was committed to protect the family against the doorman, who it was said had threatened family members with an iron bar. A coincidence? Who says magic doesn't work?

Shortly after this incident, the club management changed and the English doorman who had bad-mouthed me was arrested for selling ecstasy on the door and received a jail sentence. I do not know what became of the club manager, but it seems he too disappeared shortly afterwards.

I was quite disgusted, and vowed that I would never divulge the secrets of the craft to anyone ever again. I was somewhat dismayed that the girls seemed to enjoy the fact that they may have killed another human being through subtle means, and it was a revelation to me in a way. Power, or belief in power, is a dangerous chemical and can ignite at any given moment. Women and witchcraft are a powerful combination that no one should ever dismiss.

These girls became hardened quickly. Lexie, Martina and I seemed to represent the respectful, fluffy side of the business but when you heard some of the tales that emerged you winced. Some clubs had girls dancing for up to 16 hours a day and at all hours of the night, and it seemed that when these girls became tired the club would push stimulants on to them, creating a cycle of dependency – they had to work to get money, they needed speed to do it and the only place to get speed was through the doormen. This seemed to be a standard model with its extremes, because if girls got hooked on coke, a much more expensive drug, then of course they could be pushed into the world of vice, the only means they had of paying off large debts. Many lap-dancing clubs hire rooms in apartments near to the club for certain clients to 'unwind'. These are staffed by dancers who are picked to 'entertain' the client at extortionate cash prices, although the girl just gets her coke and a bit of cash.

In the worst of these lap-dancing establishments, the girls had to encounter drunks who would be very pushy in trying to get some form of extra. It is an old observation that drink increases the desire but dulls the chances of such acts occurring. Pushy drunks are very scary for the girls, and if the club owners and door staff don't care it can get unpleasant. Touchy, feely clients are a pain.

But the dancing girls have their own means of getting rid of idiots. It reminds me of a story I heard from a Ukrainian girl who was working in a well-known but seedy West End club. She had been ill all day, suffering from a bad case of diarrhoea, having to shower at intervals to remain clean for the strip shows. One drunken punter kept asking if he could lick her bottom, making to grab her. Finally, ill, tired and fed up, she shouted at the drunken man to stop. He took this as a sign of bravado and pulled her towards him, pushing his face into her ass – his reaction was instantaneous and he threw up on the floor, much to the amusement of the girls working that night.

But it is a hard business, and I believe that when you take bookings you are responsible for that girl's safety, and I became acutely aware that I needed security.

## The Bondage Dungeon, Brighton

The estate agent led me down some Regency stone steps into the basement flat in a less than salubrious street, boasting a halfway house, home to recovering heroin addicts, habitual drunkards, people with disturbed minds and those on bail awaiting trial. As we descended, the modern world disappeared from view. Both the worn steps and the little red-bricked patio below were strewn with rubbish; it was really squalid. Out of politeness I agreed to continue but would have happily turned back there and then. After turning the keys with some difficulty, the agent led the pair of us into a musty square ante room, where the smell of damp was evident. This little room was large enough to stash a bicycle and a few boxes, and housed the electrical cupboard, fuse box and coin meter; there was a window looking out on to the steps we had just come down. Another locked door gave access to the flat proper. This glass-panelled door was curtained, giving the flat a secure element about it. Once inside this door, it became apparent that those inside could peer through the net curtains to look outwards from the ante room.

The first part of the flat consisted of a long, wide hallway leading into a large lounge. Two closed doors were on the right of this hallway as we made our way towards the lounge. The first door on the right opened into a green bedroom of some considerable size, with a marble fireplace. Back in the hallway, the estate agent ignored the second door and led me into the lounge.

The room was 20ft x 18ft. My first impression was that it was dingy, but two large patio doors opened up on to another set of Regency stone steps, leading to a concrete patio and a back garden entrance onto another street. This was ideal for a discreet exit or quick getaway. The flat also had an ancient kitchen – the like of which I have never seen, with not even an oven – and an equally archaic bathroom with no heating, but it was at least clean.

## FIRST ENTRY – THE VIRGINAL AWAKENING

I had already made up my mind that the flat was not for me, but the estate agent had saved the best till last. I remember she opened the door gingerly to what she chose to call a study.

To fully appreciate what confronted me, you have to first imagine the smell that assailed the nostrils as soon as I stood at the threshold, composed of the overriding cloying scent of rubber with a more subtle back odour of human sweat. The poky room was no more than the size of a cell or large cupboard, its dimensions 6ft x 9ft at most with a high ceiling soundproofed with polystyrene. It was painted black and red, giving the whole room a demonic feel, and it was illuminated by a single bare lightbulb.

Placed on the ceiling were three stained wooden beams, supported by similar uprights bolted into the side walls, leaving the space free. These beams were strong and well made, possibly designed to suspend heavy objects or perhaps even people. Hooks hammered into the upright beams were obviously to assist the use of ropes and pulleys. I have to say it was very compact and had been well thought out, because there was also a lifting wooden bench, reminiscent of medieval prison beds supported by chains. This could be put down to lay someone upon or packed up at a moment's notice. On the wall was a wooden St Andrew's cross with straps attached to it. On the right-hand side, the wall had been removed so that the mirror in the adjoining bedroom could be used as a peephole. The silvering on the back of the mirror had been carefully scratched away to make a minute spyhole, but, if you stood in the bedroom, you could not have noticed it. Someone observing from the study could see into the bedroom, and it added a particularly sordid, slightly sinister dimension to the little room and its twofold purpose. The floor was solid Regency brick painted red. You could have buried a body underneath and no one would have noticed. It was clearly a fully operational bondage dungeon.

Once inside the tiny room there was absolute silence, no doubt due to the soundproofing in place, but it was uncanny. This was one of the creepiest places I have ever seen, in terms of vibes or mood. To find a room with this type of atmosphere could take decades; it was most definitely a one-off by any standards. Only the Imperial War Museum, the former Bedlam, comes anywhere near it.

The estate agent nervously awaited my answer and I left her hanging.

'This is a bondage dungeon,' I told her.

She visibly squirmed but hit back. 'It has a lot of prospective possibilities.'

At this point, I thought of having a bit of fun with her. Did she mean possibilities as a room or as a dungeon? But I was playing coy too.

'I'll give you £500 a month for the entire flat and that's my last offer.'

Some haggling took place and I prepared to walk.

'£518 a month is the lowest we'll take.'

'Done,' I said and held out my hand. We shook on the deal.

## FIRST ENTRY - THE VIRGINAL AWAKENING

I could see the relief on her face, as it was clear that no one in their right mind was going to rent such a place, but for me it had the right vibes I needed to write my next book, whatever that might be. Also, the lounge area was large enough to act as a photo studio of sorts. This place would be a goldmine. As for the dungeon, that could be turned into an office with a lick of paint and I'd soon brighten it up.

When I got the keys to the place it was empty, completely unfurnished. It was summer solstice, 21 June 2004, but the light was failing. It was here that I did a very strange thing that to this day I cannot account for. I went straight to the bondage dungeon, closed the door and stood in the pitch black. I literally drank in the darkness, as if a shadow part of myself absorbed the vibes around me. It was then I knew I'd found the right place, however grim it might be materially – I was home at last. It may have been the longest day outside but inside the darkness consoled me.

### The Photographic Agent

Within a few weeks, the place had been transformed – or at least as much as the modest budget applied to it allowed. The hallway was painted white, the carpet washed, all parts of the kitchen and bathroom scrubbed down with bleach, and the bondage dungeon was slowly dismantled, painted, its sordid peephole covered with a sticker. I left the beams up as they were bolted in tight. Some friends helped and we ended with a painting party, a BBQ in the backyard and a few drinks.

A few days on some photographic lights were brought into the flat, with tripods assembled, flash guns and so on. Lights, camera, action – it was now to be.

Work rolled in almost immediately. I took the bookings in a cheap pound-shop diary, leaving the costumes, makeup and logistics to the girls and the photography to whoever turned up to shoot. Most of it was fetish clothing, rubber dresses, bikinis and so on, or Fiona Cooper stuff – girls dressed in school ties and white blouses smoking cigarettes – the sort of thing you see in the back of some of the gutter tabloids, advertising telephone chat lines. There was definitely no porn and only one time did a sleazy photographer arrive who, after upsetting the girls with some rather seedy suggestions, was asked to leave. On the whole, the photographers were a good bunch who were respectful and paid well, often leaving tips, champagne and theatre tickets for the girls. I kept well out of the way, rarely meeting them, but I was always on site should I be needed to sling one of them out. I felt confident of being able to do that with the aid of a few 'trusty friends' – a short piece of metal tubing about the size of a Roman sword, ideal for fighting in close quarters of the hallway, the short samurai sword with razor edges, a machete, a plastic squeezy bottle of ammonia for large groups of troublemakers (as demonstrated to me by a London doorman I knew), and a loaded crossbow. These 'friends' were all close at hand. I don't know what I was expecting, but I felt confident I had more than enough in my armoury to take care of pretty much anything, even what the halfway house and co could throw at me.

## FIRST ENTRY – THE VIRGINAL AWAKENING

One day during the summer, I had left the door open to air the flat when one of the junkies from the halfway house just entered the ante room and was well into the hallway, where he spied the expensive equipment leaning against the far wall and the door leading to the lounge. I think it was too much temptation; he was walking towards it when I stepped out of the bondage dungeon-cum-office.

'Got any change, mate?' he said lamely, as we came face to face.

Although normally a compassionate man towards the needy, I knew I had to either scare him shitless or make an example of him. The alternative would be to become a soft target for him and his junkie mates. I have never regretted my decision to this day, although it is not becoming of a reverend to admit to such things. But I picked up an empty wine bottle which was lying on top of a silver flight case and broke it on the wall. I held my potential burglar by the scruff of the neck while pushing the broken bottle close into his crotch. Even in his addled state he got the message. I then threatened his brawny dealer, the big man in the street – Gogsy.

I told him that, if I was targeted, Gogsy would get bottled for starters, then I would come looking for him. I threw him away down the hallway like garbage, and he ran, thinking I was a nutter. I was one of the only people in the street who never got any trouble from the junkies. When they knew I was the Reverend, it seemed to add to the fear and several crossed the street to avoid me. It suited me. The only alternative was to lose my video equipment – and that was not going to happen. It is a bit sad that you have to be like that in modern Britain, but there are too many thieves who have no respect for community or people, and sometimes the only language they understand is fear – real or imagined. Fear of arrest, fear of reprisal.

One particular lowlife became the bane of everyone's life for a while, as he kept emptying out the communal street dustbins where people discarded their bin bags. The halfway house did nothing to stop it, although he was one of their residents. The communal bin for the whole street was almost directly outside my flat, and living in the basement meant that litter always blew down into my doorway – old coffee cups, crisp packets, fag ends, used sanitary towels and suchlike. It was not nice continually clearing it up. I warned the man doing this not to use our street, or at least to put the bags back again. It seemed I had made a mistake in being reasonable and offering the latter option, as he just saw it as a sign of weakness and continued day after day.

Finally, a Scottish man in another nearby basement who was infuriated at the problem decided to act. He too had tried to reason with him and finally exploded with extreme frustration, making a firm plan to drive the dirty scoundrel from our street. Early one morning in the autumn, he waited for litter boy to appear to do his usual trick. Sure enough, he slid back the big plastic lid of the bin and leaned right over it, reaching down for the sacks. To do this, his feet just left the ground, leaving his weight suspended on the bin. Quickly, the Scotsman moved behind him and heaved him inside. I saw him hold the lid down, then he strapped together the handle of the lid and the handle of the main body of the bin. Effectively, he had trapped the litter lout inside among the foul-smelling debris.

Litter boy shouted for release. Negotiations began. When he became threatening, a little squirt of ammonia was used to calm the situation and help perfume the inside of the bin. Within minutes a compromise was reached, but not before litter boy had thrown up.

The Scotsman unchained the bin and we went for a breakfast together, never giving it another thought. Extreme though this seems, after this incident our street was one of the few at the seafront without the persistent problem of junkie litter beggars and antisocial types. I had learned from the Albanians, when in the presence of wolves, never be a lamb.

Similarly, the Scotsman also had other methods of keeping the peace. In winter, when it was minus five or so, a band of junkies would often be screaming at the top of their voices to be let into the halfway house at 4 a.m., without regard for working people sleeping. Doors would be kicked in, windows were broken, bottle fights would break out, overdose candidates were kicked into the gutter with nary a police car to move them on. It was a disgrace. The Scotsman would just go out and empty a bucket of cold water over the offenders; they tended not to hang around in the wintry cold much after that, for fear of catching pneumonia. It was a hard street to live in and you either stood up for yourself or got shafted. I saw things in that seedy little street that I had never seen before, as well as learning a helluva lot about life.

Of course, there were good sides too; the Brighton hoteliers were always friendly, and at Christmas would invite you in for a drink or two. The local boozer, the Lion and Lobster, affectionately known as the Lion and Lob-on, was probably one of the best in the town, with plenty of live music, lovely food and even lovelier women. A backpackers' hostel in the street saw a steady supply of travellers and there were some great parties, particularly in the summer. Being near to the old pier, beach life was fantastic in the summer and even in the autumn months. With a vibrant social scene, music at all hours, beautiful bohemian people, clubbing, beach BBQs, surfing, sand and samba, Brighton life never seemed to stop. Sleep always seemed to be the last thing on my mind.

I quietly went about my own business with complete discretion, gradually filling up my paltry bank account. I could hardly believe it, but the flat was paying its way. Everyone was content. These were, I realise now, halcyon days in the most unlikely of circumstances. Not until the monotonous idyll was shattered did my real journey begin. A fresh business proposition had been offered and, as the girls' modelling agent, I took the train from Brighton to King's Cross, with the hope of renewed fortunes.

# CHAPTER 2

# STRAPPED
# FOR CASH

## The Sweet Smell of Success

A piss-wreaking wreck of a man descended from the Euston Station escalator, gripped my hand sweatily and weakly, but shook it enthusiastically, making it feel like more of a wank than a handshake – a waft of stale urine followed. Enter Steve 'the Spank'. Quite taken aback, I was gripped on to by a man in his late fifties, short, squat and sporting an outdated grey flannel suit complemented by a grey-ginger Jimmy Edwards moustache and sideburns. If this wasn't bad enough, Steve suffered from chronic dandruff, bad breath, rotten teeth and a heavily flushed face – evidence of acute alcoholism.

Apart from his broad Yorkshire accent, most pronounced of all was Steve's unmistakable waddle caused by elephantitus which had caused a huge growth of his pelvis, slowing his walk. As this peculiar specimen waddled beside me, the stench of urine was only dulled by the smell of stale alcohol. Steve the Spank was a living medical textbook on legs, and one could only wonder what sort of degenerate life had led to this pitiful physical cul-de-sac. But I found Steve fascinating. In hindsight, I must say that this was to be my real introduction to the British spanking industry, from a past master. Steve's personality was upbeat, his banter jovial and peppered with a fair helping of acid wit, sure-fire one-liners and a general repartee that overcame his obvious physical downside. He was a man buzzing with coarse jokes, brilliant one-liners and a bunch of easy money-making schemes, all thrown together with a certain Northern charm. Most people who met Steve immediately got on with him and I was no exception.

Talk of winning racehorses dominated the conversation, and it was clear Steve was a consummate professional among gamblers of all sorts. His commercial interests included horses and online casinos as well as other forms of gambling, particularly cards on the net. Steve, however, had a passion even greater than gambling, which punctuated all of his dealings. This was Mr Mercury, a quicksilver surfer with a fistful of porn ideas – easy money transfers, publishing coups, fast, lucrative downloads – but, sadly, he'd put none of them into practice. Steve was also a serial conman, and, like most who had been seduced early on, I was not able to see beyond his carefully constructed, likeable façade.

## STRAPPED FOR CASH

Over a steaming curry at King's Cross Tandoori, I downed an early glass of red wine and was grateful for the bouquet that, thankfully, drowned out the wafts of urine which drifted my way from time to time. The lamb tikka masala also helped. Steve was evidently a curry aficionado, ordering something ostentatiously hot like vindaloo or chicken phal.

Over our second and third bottles of red, Steve finally came to his full powers, talking quickly without pause. 'I own the largest single collection of school uniforms in the world, currently listed as 5000 full sets. That is blazer, shirt, skirt and socks. Of course, some are multiples and some can be made from taking a white shirt from another as required; many ties are interchangeable but of late I have turned my attention to South African schools. Now take your regulation knickers, for example, in South Africa they have to be worn in certain combinations and at various term times. I have collected the school prospectuses, you know, and I'll be putting those out on the net for twenty bucks a throw.'

The flow of detailed information concerning school uniform rules and regulations, the height of skirts above the knee, the right height for the heels on the girls' shoes and what summer blazer was worn at a particular school continued – Steve was a veritable bottomless pit of information that he had crafted into five niche magazines. The titles of these publications left nothing to the imagination: *Uniform Collector*, *Uniform Girls*, *Uniform Special*, *Uniform Discipline*, etc. Later, as porn-magazine publishing declined in favour of the web, Steve augmented these titles with similar-genre websites featuring such themes as regulation knickers, with a much-celebrated 'knicker tour', uniform discipline and the fantasy of punished schoolgirls (naturally 18+, I hasten to add). As Steve's nickname suggested, all the female models involved in his photography were spanked in traditional classroom settings, or reformatories in some cases. To this end, the photo stories employed a wide variety of implements from gym shoes to rulers and the school cane, Steve's favourite.

'You've got to appreciate that the real punter, and I mean the die-hard punter, has got to get off. So, in the case of South Africa, everyone knows they are still spanking in schools. It has got to be a pull. Genuine uniforms with genuine punishments – South African style. It has the hallmark of authenticity about it and the punter will always pay for the real thing.' He grinned and chinked my glass in a toast to imagined success.

Before I could say cheers, he was off again at breakneck speed. In his thick Yorkshire brogue, he explained his interest in the girls he had seen advertised on the internet. 'Now Martina has subs. Subs are gold dust in this game; forget the doms, it's all about subs. Anyone can wield a cane but taking one is another matter and I pride myself on being as sub as I am dom. I wouldn't dish out what I wasn't prepared to take myself and that includes the cane. Now, Martina not only has subs, but she has two South African subs …' He paused for effect. 'So there is a bit of business to be done here and everyone benefits.'

Here his hand began to make sweeping, dramatic gestures suggesting a vista of easy riches. 'Think of it as a federal arrangement where everyone is pulling in cash from punters; each one of us has his or her own expertise and I am willing to pitch in and take the photographs and develop them for free,' he offered generously.

I flicked through the magazine he had given me from his *Uniform* series. The photos were indeed well composed and the uniforms very authentic, as were the locations.

As one might imagine, I was a little lost for words at the meeting, as I had thought he had just come to hire a model or two, but did manage to proffer, 'Where is this location? It seems like a real school, please don't tell me ...'

'Oh, that's Judy's school. My wife runs an authentic 1950s school, complete with old-fashioned wooden desks, you know, with ink wells, and traditional maps of the world shaded with the vast territories of the British Empire; there is even an authentic gym with climbing bars and vaulting horse.' Steve stabbed a finger across the table towards one of the pages. 'And that is Judy.'

I blinked in disbelief, perhaps registering my shock, as Judy was a very attractive woman in her late forties who probably went to the gym (the real one) and certainly seemed to take great care over her appearance. What she saw in Steve I could not fathom. In all honesty, I found it completely bewildering, perhaps even more so than everything else I had heard or seen to date, and it left me almost speechless.

'It is located in an industrial unit in Wakefield,' Steve said proudly. 'Between me and our Judy we cover all bases. Genuine school CP. Now you can begin to see the federal arrangement I'm talking about. A real tour-de-force that. We could be looking at something of a renaissance in British spanking today – with young South African subs on board, we're on starter's orders.' Steve smiled, stroking his Jimmy Edwards sideburn on one side.

As several large flakes of dandruff made their way across the table on to the naan bread, I felt a little sick.

### The Last Days of Innocence

Martina handed me £60 towards expenses as Steve had stitched me up for the meal, making some lame excuse for not carrying cash in such a dangerous area. To be honest, I had been glad to get out of the restaurant at the end, not caring for bills or who paid them. Fresh air was king and I drank in the revitalising ozone from the vista of Brighton seafront.

Martina had been patient for the debrief but could hold on no more. 'What happened with this man Steve? Is he a good man?'

'He seems a nice guy but it's a weird set-up,' I answered vaguely, staring from the promenade into the churning waves.

'Oh, come on, Jon, you were there.' Martina wanted answers.

I snapped back to reality. 'Well, his wife has got a school for adults up North; it is very real with desks, blackboards and even an old gym. They use it for filming and have made about 30 films there. Steve has produced five magazines and about the same number of websites and he wants to do some business with you and the girls.' As I tried to sum up the meeting, the memory of the smell of stale urine burned back into my mind.

'So what are we to do with him?' Martina was being very Polish and practical.

I nearly answered, 'Give him a fucking good scrub,' but the words came mechanically: 'He has proposed that a new school-spanking website is set up and he's offering to pay for it, maintain it, take the photos and develop them, and to film a limited amount of video clips in return for half of the revenue. Most of the sites take an average of £300 per week minus the exes, so say £270 per week on each site – that's around £135 your share.'

'It doesn't seem like a lot of money. Is it much work?'

'Well, Steve thinks with video on an SMS download this sum could be quite a lot more. Then he has mentioned doing his parties in the North, maybe setting up some in the South too. I guess it's an experiment. He is keen on the South African girls really, because he has South African school-uniform scenarios planned.' I tried to keep it all simple.

'He's not a paedophile, is he? England seems to be full of them at the moment.'

Martina may not have asked the question that seriously, but it was the first time I had even thought about it. An avid collector of school uniforms, obsessed with caning schoolgirls, albeit adult ones, and producing magazines with Lolita-style adults in educational or institutional settings. My mouth must have been gaping.

'Anyway, I am 24 and out of danger,' she said, laughing.

'No, I think he is just a businessman but a very perverted one.'

It was my turn to smile. Thankfully, the conversation moved on to something else for a while. But I was aware that Steve was waiting in the wings. Like most nightmarish situations it began quite innocently. The person who first uttered that the road to hell was paved with good intentions deserves all credit.

On the eve of Steve's visit to Brighton, all the necessary arrangements, bar one, had been made. However, the photography studio had fallen through at the last minute, leaving the big problem of where to do the shoots. Martina and the girls came to my flat, where an anxious debate ensued about using my bondage dungeon-cum-office for the shoot. As much as I wanted to help, I didn't want to get more deeply involved.

I paced up and down in the large basement lounge, as Martina sat silent and several of the girls sat frowning and scowling

'I am not allowing my place to be used for filming this man's photography. It is my office and I am not moving everything to accommodate this shoot,' I said defiantly. 'I have told you all before I become too involved.'

'But you *are* involved. You pitched the deal, remember?' came the immediate reply from one of the scowlers, a blonde Afrikaner with a fiery temper whom we'll call Giesla.

'It is true that I brokered the deal on your behalf; it is also true that I have minded you all, negotiated, driven you places, suggested ideas, helped you all in every way I can to see you through your fledgling business. But this photo shoot – I am not doing it and that's final.' I stopped pacing and faced Martina, as the wind outside whipped the building as if in readiness for the scourging and belting to be meted out the following day.

'You're a stubborn fucker, just like my fucking dad,' said Fran, one of the other girls, trying in vain to inject some humour into the sombre clique of models.

'I know he wants to film us all outdoors, some photos in a park, some at the swings, but the weather is bad and if he comes all this way what are we to tell him?' Martina asked.

Martina's sad brown eyes and straight delivery always swayed my judgement.

'You can keep the uniforms in here and change in this room if you want – think of it as a Winnebago – but no snaps and that's my last word on it.'

But my last word didn't keep anyone quiet and a cacophony of voices rose up. Martina kept silent.

'This room is bigger than the bondage dungeon – why can't we use this one? You know Martina will give you big Rand for it.' Giesla was picking a fight and lit yet another cigarette. 'Why no photos? You've done other shoots here before.'

Another shrieked, 'How can we work like this? You're not helping at all!'

I threw up my hands in despair, feeling a spike of anger pushing through my thinning layers of patience. What part of 'no' did they not understand?

Martina stood and the room went quiet. She never lost her cool. 'If Jon wants it that way, we should listen and do it that way. This is a chance for us to do something new and we can give it our best attention. Right, girls? The weather may be good. After all, we are doing it for free, right? Let us try, OK.'

All the girls sort of nodded and then said yes. Martina commanded not only their respect but also their undying loyalty. I was thankful for the rescue and went off hunting for alcohol in the form of extra-large Guinness cans. Models would drive anyone to drink, as any agent will tell you; it is certainly not easy money.

Only when I had been fortified by a can and a half did I return to find most of the girls had left. Martina smiled at me, put her hand gently on my shoulder and said goodbye. Like everyone else I really respected Martina, who was ice cool – the linchpin of the entire operation. I just prayed she wasn't downwind from Steve on the shoot, as she would never forgive me for it.

## On Location

A blustery May morning saw Steve waddle out on to Brighton platform carrying two bulky leather suitcases, camera around his neck, looking like someone visiting for a touch of Dr Brighton – medicinal sea airs, tourist shots and perhaps just a bit of slap and tickle on the side. In reality, he was there just for the slap. Little did innocent fellow passengers realise, as they walked beside him along the railway terminus, that he was armed with leather paddles, straps and canes, as well as a variety of carefully wrapped uniforms in preparation for some very naughty pictures.

Once inside the car, his familiar fragrance permeated the

atmosphere. I wound down the window to take advantage of the blustery winds.

Steve quickly announced, 'My hotel has informed me that my room has been double-booked and I may have to stop at yours. You don't mind, do yer? Sounds like the photo studio is just the same. Is it always like this in Brighton? One of the girls said you had a spare settee. Well, it keeps costs down anyway, doesn't it?' Steve didn't wait for an answer but continued on about his vision for a great federal arrangement spanning the entire spanking scene.

I didn't listen too closely as the wind from the open window kept drowning him out, but remembered that I had an inflatable plastic bed I could put him on, which perhaps could be thrown away if it was impregnated by his stench.

'I'll pick up some wine, and could you drop me at the bookies because I couldn't get a bet on at King's Cross? My train times were too tight. Got to have a quick nip, though. Excuse me, won't you?' Steve produced a silver hip flask and gulped down whatever was inside. 'Now let's organise a shoot at the park with Martina and I'll get some stills of her in uniform at Brighton Station.'

I nearly swerved the car in shock. Events were moving at a fast pace.

'You'll be coming along to assist, won't you?'

'The railway station?' I tried to sound au fait with it all, but sounded sheepish instead.

'Well, of course. There's nothing like getting these girls in traditional uniform and parading them in natural settings like railway stations, libraries or even high tea in one of the prestigious hotels. Is the Grand in Brighton?' He looked at me mischievously, but I knew he wasn't joking. 'The punters want to see them out there, regulation knickers and all, in real-life situations. It's no good hiding your light under a bushel, is it?'

I was not amused, and certainly was not about to walk behind a girl in school uniform and her somewhat dubious photographer. There were limits. After all, I knew people in Brighton. I felt a surge of righteous Victorian hypocrisy and said no.

'A federal arrangement demands planning and dare. Now, I'll have the two South African subs at the playground; I need swings, slide and climbing frame.'

'A children's playground? Are you sure that's wise? Brighton is a small place, you know. People might get the wrong idea.' An unsettled feeling gnawed in the pit of my stomach. What had I let myself in for? I thought SJ took the piss, hiring army depots and church halls for his films, but these suggestions had taken matters to an altogether different level. 'No, I can't do it, Steve. Sorry.'

My passenger gulped the remaining dregs of his hip flask, clearly unworried by my lack of faith.

After stopping at the bookies and the off-licence and dropping off his bags, we parked the car and went to the Lion and Lobster. True to form, Steve plumped for good old bangers and mash with lashings of gravy. It seemed this man was a traditionalist in every respect.

## STRAPPED FOR CASH

'Now a lot of people may say that corporal punishment is an assault. That is the way politically correct society sees it, but no, if anyone came to me and said it is an assault or some such nonsense, my reply would be this: corporal punishment, particularly caning, is part of our heritage.' Steve nodded defiantly. 'It is a tradition – a very English, no, *British* tradition and we should be proud of it. The colonies took to it; I mean, just look at Malaysia, Singapore, Australia and South Africa, of course. Where is our little township girl today, anyway?'

'I wouldn't start calling her that. She's white Afrikaans,' I said, trying to head off any potential flashpoints, as I was sure Giesla would have walked out if he spoke to her like that. There was enough trouble brewing without having to deal with any political issues.

Thankfully, the food arrived and Steve attacked it as before, ordering copious amounts of red wine. During lunch, he became very witty and I relaxed a bit. We laughed and drank and got drunk. It was quite a pleasant afternoon, despite the occasional waft of Steve's own brand of perfume. We had consumed nearly two bottles of red each. Steve wasn't even touched by it and went out for a late scotch. Understandably, no filming took place that day.

Later, Steve found his way on to the plastic inflatable bed, clean sheets and all. I took refuge in the furthest reaches of the large flat to await Martina's early arrival the following day.

In the morning, I felt jaded but Steve was buzzing about, making ready with cameras and film stock, not to mention busily

53

unpacking an array of uniforms. Martina arrived and within minutes she'd changed into the school uniform. It was a blue and red striped blazer, straw boater hat, blue shirt, grey V-neck jumper, navy-blue skirt and grey socks with a pair of very conservative black shoes.

I drove the pair to the back of the railway station and let them walk off and do the deed. To me it seemed crazy, but to my relief they returned happily 20 minutes later. According to Martina, no one had been interested in them. Next it was off to a country park, where thankfully no one was in sight. Here Steve practically doubled over his Minolta camera, snapping away avidly. His elephantitus obviously provided some sort of counterbalance to his huge fat frame, allowing him a surprising degree of dexterity. The day was turning out well. Martina's shoot had seemed effortless. Soon she was gone and it was Fran's and Giesla's turn to change into their yellow and brown uniforms. Then it was off to the playground, just as Steve had planned, leaving me feeling like an accomplice to some sordid perverted act. The feeling of dread at the railway station was nothing compared to this.

I pleaded with them to change their minds but they all laughed at me. My mind could not comprehend what sort of punter would want to see young girls in school uniform in a playground. Was this spanking porn? Nonce, the word for a child-sex offender, came to mind.

Steve encouraged it all and became very eager, as if half the fun was taking these extraordinary risks. But again my paranoia proved unfounded and nothing happened. I put it down to the streets being deserted. In fact, this time no one at all witnessed the extraordinary spectacle, yet it was as brazen as could be.

Puffed up with confidence, Steve went on to meet the final model, a tall, dark Slovakian girl called Mariana, also dressed in yellow and brown. She was due to be caned hard across her regulation knickers, inside my hallway of all places, despite my serious misgivings, then driven on to a netball court where, as she jumped up knickerless, her cane marks would be exposed. I told him straight away that I was not going to be anywhere near this shoot and that I totally disapproved. I even tried to talk some sense into him in order to dissuade him from doing this crazy thing.

Mariana arrived punctually and said matter-of-factly, 'Let's get the caning out of the way. Lay it on hard as I don't want to do it again, OK?'

I still wanted to say they couldn't do it here, but fear of them doing it elsewhere gripped my heart. I made an excuse and went to the shops for some milk.

As fate would have it, Steve completely went to pieces when he started the punishment, witnessed by five other girls of all nationalities. Upon my return, a rather distressed Steve pulled me to one side and said, 'She is a dom not a sub, I can't do it.'

The girl was ordered to change immediately and gave him a strange glance in return. He immediately cancelled the rest of the day's shoot for the cover of the pub and I was not going to stop him, as I thought he was a bit of a loose cannon to say the least.

Mariana admitted, while changing, that she hated working as a submissive and much preferred the thought of being a dom, and that Steve had detected something deep inside her; it was quite natural for her to want to hurt people in love play. How had Steve known this? She left wondering about the incident herself and decided to quit the business shortly afterwards.

### The Mancunian Candidate

At the Lion and Lobster, the meal this time was Irish stew washed down with a different red wine. The pub was always convivial, and, at the time, it was frequented by a number of famous porn models.

In his cups, Steve decreed that the final shoot was to be Brighton beach itself – the promenade by the old pier. The stupid prick had chosen the nearest spot possible to my flat, and part of me thought that there might be an element of *schadenfreude* behind it. He really enjoyed my discomfort but then of course he was a sado-masochist. I declared that as I would not be needed I would have a lie-in instead. My patience was already wearing thin on me.

The two South African girls laughed wildly at Steve's jokes; they loved every second of it but I was beginning to have second thoughts about Steve. He had made a curious remark on the car journey home about the punters who bought his magazines: 'Never give a sucker an even break.' It was not very nice and it was the first time I wondered if this hail-fellow-well-met photographer could really be trusted after all. During the meal, he also started to make little snide comments about other websites, editors of other publications and certain models. It was this subtle change of tone, perhaps rather trifling in retrospect, that made me wonder if his mask was slipping. I was going to watch this smooth-talking man like a hawk from now on.

Dutifully, the two South African models set off with Steve at 7.10 a.m. sharp the next morning, walking out into a cold, damp sea mist rolling off the beach. I had given a stark warning that they were to be back no later than 8.30 a.m., as walkers, joggers and the like would soon appear at that time and were sure to get involved. I stressed that they should just get the photos done and return. As a precaution, the girls took long overcoats to disguise their school uniforms, the yellow and brown number again. Nonetheless, I watched them go with some trepidation.

At 9 a.m., I answered the door to two rather serious-looking police officers who had Giesla with them.

'There has been an incident on the beach,' said the Mancunian-sounding police constable, who also informed me that Fran had been detained at the beach with Steve.

'Photographs by any chance?' I asked matter-of-factly.

'Yes. Do you know this young lady? And, more to the point, her age?'

'Yeah, I know her. She's 19. Why?'

'Are you sure? Because we have an incident.'

'What is the problem, officer?' I tried to take charge of the situation, but it was obviously something serious as both officers were becoming somewhat belligerent towards me, demanding to come in, asking me all sorts of loaded questions. My heart sank.

'They think I am underage, Jon.'

'We'll deal with this, miss.'

'What do you want here, officer?'

'We'd like to see this lady's passport, and we understand both girls got changed here in this house.' The WPC seemed to be calming down a bit.

'Well, that's simple, isn't it? Let the girl get her passport and inspect it.'

'We need to come in with her,' said the Mancunian. He wasn't letting up and virtually forced his way into the flat.

Within ten seconds, the passport was produced and the situation should have been resolved. Then the sorry story emerged. At precisely 8.45 a.m., a member of the public walking their dog had seen Steve kneeling down taking up-skirt shots of two 'schoolgirls' on the beach. Understandably, suspicions of paedophilia had been raised at the station and two constables, a sergeant and an inspector, plus two squad cars, had been dispatched to the crime scene. I shook my head in dismay. I could just picture Steve in full flow not giving a damn about the public, perving over the regulation knickers.

Why had I been so foolish as to allow it to happen? The worst thing was I got a lecture about paedophilia from the moronic constable who stood before me. It was about all I could take; hungover and stressed by the situation, I vented my full spleen on the unfortunate Mancunian. He tried to argue but I waved him away, furious, and asked him to leave immediately. His colleague saw that I wasn't interested in what they had to say and they left.

Bitterly regretting the day I had ever laid eyes on Steve the Spank, I went berserk, cutting up the plastic inflatable bed with a machete. I felt ready to meet Steve again.

Half-an-hour later, Steve returned looking sheepish, all his bluster and blarney gone. Awkwardly, he offered the ridiculous excuse that the Lancastrian police officer disliked him just because he was a Yorkshireman.

'I had an office in Manchester, St Caths area. They'll always go for a Yorkshireman. It's the War of the Roses, you know,' Steve said morosely. I think he knew instinctively that he was washed up with me.

Later, I rebuffed his offer of a quick drink before he caught the train home. He looked as he really was for the first time – a very weak, ill, sick man with possibly no life beyond spanking, a social pariah of whom no good could ultimately come. He looked beaten. I drove him back to the station in virtual silence. He had strode around only a day or two before in perverted glee; now he was somewhat sobered by his recent brush with the law. It was the last time that I saw Steve the Spank in person but it was not to end there. Like the wings of an Amazon butterfly whose fluttering causes a subtle breeze which, in turn, increases to cause a great storm, we would all reap the whirlwind.

One of the most surprising things I learned about Steve during my time with him was that, despite his hedonistic lifestyle, he was a deeply religious man. I can only wonder what he would have been like if he was godless.

## *Deliverance from Evil*

An emergency meeting was held by Martina and the girls to decide what to do in light of Steve's stupidity. A split vote meant that the team took the reluctant but calculated risk that, as the photos had already been taken, they should carry on working with Steve. They felt committed.

From now on, Steve rang every day at nine o'clock on the dot to give progress reports as the girls continued their fetish work. A spanking website appeared but it had old photos on it. Martina and the girls were never featured. Steve promised revenue but nothing materialised. A webcam was offered but, during installation, he claimed that the company had rolled back the start date. Suspicions about him were rising, as more promises were made but he delivered nothing.

Then, out of the blue, he asked Fran, his favourite South African model, up to Wakefield to attend a spanking party hosted by Judy at her school, attended by members of the public. For a time, it seemed as Steve had just about salvaged his reputation by landing this gig.

However, it all went wrong when Fran was four hours late on her train. It isn't clear what had happened, although the more cynical models thought it was a case of a classic E comedown with a couple of hours' snooze on the train. It appeared Steve viewed her late arrival as some sort of revenge on him. Judy was not a happy camper and insisted on inflicting a public punishment caning in front of the whole party. Fran claimed later that this led to a fling with the severe headmistress in her private quarters. Whatever actually happened that day we shall never know, but it seemed that Steve's world of control was creaking at the seams, with the unfortunate news that the last of his magazines were to cease being printed. Martina began to wonder what was going on money-wise – she'd received nothing as yet. It was beginning to seem like looking down into a huge great crater at dawn; slowly, each and every crevice is exposed as the light increases, every huc and colour emerges – and so with the conman time gradually illuminates his scheming ways.

The entire chapter may have passed without further incident and been put down to bad business – were it not for Steve's notebook containing a long list of email addresses, which the girls found in Fran's suitcase when she returned from the Wakefield spanking party.

After wondering how the book had got there, Fran finally remembered that Steve had dropped it while stumbling around her room, pissed out of his skull. Through sheer curiosity, the girls looked at the book.

It was clear that its contents were part of a scam, but they couldn't quite fathom what it was all about. However, they knew the canny Martina would be sure to fill in the missing jigsaw pieces, and they lost no time getting on the phone to her. The book contained a list of names of all the people who had responded to a party advertisement using the pictures of Fran. It seemed Steve had collected the details but not passed them on to Martina. It is not on record what Martina actually said, but within the hour she was in possession of the list and on the phone to me. Martina had immediately prepared a BCC reply to all 78 names, asking whether they had received the party details.

Forty minutes later, the first replies came in demanding their £50 deposits back. It was a scam and Steve had used Martina's name. Hell hath no fury like a woman scorned, and I could hear the war drums pounding. Martina texted me to tell me that she was now organising her own spanking party using the scam database. It was to be called Spankaholics. It smelled heavily of irony but nothing was said. She announced that most of the email complaints had been successfully dealt with and that she was looking for her own venue in London.

Within days, Martina had found a suitable location in the West End, near Warren Street tube station, which was only too happy to book in five girls for a private gentlemen's spanking party. A firm date was set and now all that was left to do was to advertise the party on a couple of fetish information websites, to alert everyone of the date. A new party was in town: Spankaholics!

However, as quickly as the advert went up, it was pulled down again. Martina tried a second time but the same thing happened. She rang the webmaster and the response was blunt: if you are in league with Steve the Spank, we don't want you. She found herself talking to a dialling tone.

It was time for some decisive action in the form of a few choice calls – one to the fetish webmaster, Mick, and the other to Steve. Martina asked me to do the honours.

When I rang Mick to fully explain our position with the largely discredited Steve, and the truthful extent of our involvement with him, I was met with some guarded cynicism. It was natural enough, as the poor man was owed over £1000 by Steve and wasn't going to be taken in again. While Mick sympathised with us, he did warn me that we were joining a long line of 'creditors', as he termed it, including himself, and told me that Steve was a proper conman. It appeared many others had succumbed to the dubious charms of the Spank. In fact, others we found later wanted to kill him, and it seemed an attempt had already been made on his life in Hereford, when a car driven by a certain pony master and transvestite, who was also an ex-mercenary, had mounted the pavement.

But the real bombshell came when Mick announced that Steve was also Martin, and sometimes Paul, and there were a host of surnames and pseudonyms to match.

Having thanked Mick for his candour, I made the next very necessary phone call. I rang Steve and told him that we no longer wished to do business with him. He knew immediately he had been rumbled.

As the weeks went by, many more allegations emerged; some of the claims were almost amusing, like the one where he had supposedly exchanged labels on bottles of cheap Pomagne with champagne bottles, but other stories were not so funny and had apparently left people penniless.

The piece de resistance was a frantic phone call from Steve's 'wife' Judy, claiming that, in fact, she had never been married to Steve at all and that he had taken her for £8,000 shortly after the Martina incident. Yorkshire Police had been called after the pair fell out and Judy was said to have made serious death threats against him.

My next call was to the transvestite who had apparently tried to run Steve over in Hereford. There were clearly no regrets here, as he still expressed a strong desire to take an axe to Steve's head if he ever laid eyes on him again. The transvestite, now deceased, had apparently never given up his search for the elusive photographer.

If anyone naively thought this would be the last of Steve the Spank, they were sorely mistaken. He would continue to prove to be a pain, but more of that later.

The ever-professional Martina worked hard on her parties, and, in less than two years, managed to save over £50,000 from spanking. It was a bitter blow when she announced she was returning to her profession as an engineer and was quitting the UK to further her career with a large conglomerate on the Continent.

We had a goodbye party in Brighton in an oriental-themed gay bar. It was low key, with a glass of red wine, some hugs and a fond embrace. But it was really over. Lexie disappeared soon after.

## STRAPPED FOR CASH

After taking stock of my options, I felt there seemed little point in being a model agent now, plus a couple of people I had known were embroiled in scandals that made me seriously reassess the seedy world of spanking porn. And anyway, I wanted to write an all-encompassing book – it was time to move on.

I quit as the girls' agent and decided to go into the far more lucrative world of buying and selling films. Distribution is a whole new ocean of possibility but, of course, it also has bigger sharks.

It was an open road out there for me. So I put my foot to the pedal, and did what I do best. I returned to the world of video.

# CHAPTER 3

# WOULD THE REAL GODDESS PLEASE COME FORWARD?

### *Her Majesty Requests ...*

I now wanted to know the other side of pain, from the viewpoint of those who dish it out, and I was introduced to a nice African girl aged about 30, whom we shall call Mistress Sardar. Her name is unimportant because she regularly assumed the mantle of a living goddess, which I liked.

A few days after being introduced we hooked up. As I made my way downstairs into the gloomy maisonette in north London, my nostrils were assailed by the pungent aroma of expensive perfume and rubber and, within that mix, the scent of talcum powder. Mistress Sardar was a dark beauty of West African origin, dressed in a Shirley Bassey wig, a tight PVC dress and knee-length high-heel black boots with laces right up to the top, carrying a riding crop. She greeted me with a great smile, her scarlet-glossed lips sparkling in the gloom, and bade me to come into her lair. So this was a fully functioning dungeon, not like the old shell back in Brighton.

But before I was treated to a good look, I was introduced to the aging maid and the bouncer, a rather meaty ex-soldier called Freddy in his early fifties. They were pleasant enough but they looked world-weary, lacklustre, as if they were time-served old hands at the game. Sardar whisked me away as the odd couple returned to their afternoon-television chat show.

I followed Mistress Sardar further into the back of the building, as, strutting confidently, she led me into the dungeon which was stacked high with every known instrument of pain and pleasure imaginable. Some of the devices were forbidding, even frightening, as she gave me a half-mocking, half-serious guided tour of her establishment. I dressed so squarely it was almost like America's 1950s meets the acid generation, but I was acutely aware that you should never judge a book by its cover. PVC was definitely haute couture in these circles and very much *in*, while looking normal – or vanilla, as fetish people would say – was *out*.

Once inside the dungeon, Sardar's spiel began with a thick wooden cross, a ubiquitous torture instrument, which was palmed off quickly. 'This is the St Andrew's cross. A bit staid but the slaves like it. Not very adventurous though.'

She looked at me, beginning to turn a black metal device while at the same time gauging my reaction. 'This is the cradle –

it allows you to strap up a slave and turn them around 360. Fancy a spin?'

I shook my head. Sardar smiled and let out a great shriek of joy.

Moving to one side, she looked down. After stroking a black box with a German SS sign on it, she gently sprang it open to reveal a glass pipe attached to some wires. I thought it might be an enema but Sardar carefully explained it was an electrical torture device. Upon closer inspection, I saw the ominous-looking dials for increasing both ampage and voltage. I backed away from the malevolent contraption.

'We'll be having some fun with this later,' she said, smiling broadly.

There were several benches where a client could be strapped facedown or supine, so they could be dealt with accordingly. Nearby half-melted candles hinted at one of the tortures that could be applied. On the wall over the bench hung a ball-gag, no doubt to stifle the screams, and alongside it a huge array of whips, crops and lashes graced the wall. Most of the furniture was black or red, *de rigueur* in all self-respecting bondage dungeons.

The centrepiece of the dungeon was a high chair, crafted in leather and studwork. It was mighty and majestic and purple – the only piece of furniture not following the red/black theme.

'This is not for slaves, only the Mistress sits here,' I was informed firmly. 'This is the Queening Throne. Only I sit here. Would you be interested in filming that?'

'If you like,' I answered non-committally.

'So you're a voyeur then?' She laughed at me and winked.

'No way. I was just curious, that's all. Because you make it sound so special.' My tone of voice was already justifying myself and I was slightly annoyed at my reaction.

Her face became serious. 'It *is* special, you see. It is where my slaves meet their Goddess. I reward them by allowing the slaves to lick my boots, or suck each other off in my presence. If I am feeling generous then I may transform to give them a full Queening session. But they have to be very obedient to get that rare treat.'

'Don't they just pay you for your services and demand whatever *they* want?' I thought I was pushing her out of her comfort zone, but she was quick to counteract my impertinent question.

'Not at all.' She looked at me haughtily. 'The clients who come here do see other Mistresses, but none of them offers the reward of the Queening Throne. It is something I make my slaves work towards. Not anyone can just come here and demand it. I would never allow it for a start!' She moved closer, smiling and flexing the whip. 'I want you to see the true Goddess in me. I want you there at the Queening session. When Georgina and Alana come, I want you to film it. Yes. Film it!' She laughed wildly and it filled the bondage dungeon.

I liked Mistress Sardar; she was fun, although I suspected she could be a bit of a handful if you got on the wrong side of her.

Freddy had filed in silently behind us and was lurking in the doorway. 'Film it? Why?' he said plainly.

She turned and glared at him. 'I want Jon here with us, that's why. It will be useful for my other slaves on the website to see a film of me in my full supremacy and domination.' Turning back to me, Sardar smiled sweetly. 'Yes, film it, Jon, please. Prepare for a full Queening session. I want to play Goddess today. Freddy, clean the throne and sterilise everything.'

'Yes, Mistress.' The ex-soldier almost snapped to attention.

Sardar strutted out of the room and Freddy turned his back to me to leave. 'You better get your camera, mate. You've got two hours before the punters arrive.'

When nobody rejoined me, I realised it was the end of the meeting and left the building in search of camera, lights and tapes.

I looked at my watch – the whole meeting had only taken nine minutes but seemed like an hour. It seemed to me that bondage dungeons had their own time/space continuum. They are strange places. Perhaps they are the modern temples to the flesh, places of worship – Goddess worship?

## Sex, Slaves, Puke and Video Tape

The lights were up and functioning, the two small cameras were in place and the still camera in hand. All was set for the slaves' arrival. They filed in silently: Alan/Alana, who was in his early forties, and George/Georgina, the elder of the pair, who was pushing fifty.

Their story unfolded over a cigarette. For the past decade, both men had, in their own inimitable way, beaten a path deep

**71**

into the S&M scene, and it had been a very bold step to make their years of fantasy real. Their tale may seem familiar to some. It started with masturbation in their youth wearing women's clothes, then came their girlfriends' makeup, then paying to visit a dominatrix, or even having long-term mistresses who would act on a paid retainer when the kinky desires needed to be sated. Gradually, their fetish lifestyles increased their visits to bondage parlours, rubber balls, whipping sessions, toilet training and participation in orgiastic parties dressed in PVC or leather, until their extreme sexual acts reached maturity. The fantasy no longer existed; they had become individualised. Fetish had become as normal as catching the tube to the City.

Here we were at that point, and it was normal – as normal as anything I have ever encountered. Alana and Georgina were nice guys – there was no passion, no heat, nothing could be further from extreme. But then what is extreme?

I did not pry, but Alan volunteered that he had worked in the City before having a nervous breakdown and now spent his days as an insurance actuary. George was a wizened, greying, almost emaciated, nervy character, who worked with trust funds. Both men were above-average earners, with all the trappings of that lifestyle: pads in nice parts of London, country pieds-a-terre, yachting breaks and holidays in exotic parts. Their secret outlet, their drug of choice if you like, was to visit one of London's mistresses – Sardar.

And now here we all were, standing around chatting while Sardar changed.

## WOULD THE REAL GODDESS PLEASE COME FORWARD?

The pair were clearly nervous of being on film but had been ordered to take part by Sardar. I assured them it was just for fun and the Mistress could have the tape at the end. I would endeavour not to show their faces during the action. Meekly they nodded, already beginning to transform their moods and personality for the action ahead. They were getting into character.

Sardar suddenly marched into the room, her gait exuding power. She was glowing, cheeks rouged, head held high, shoulders back and very much in control. Her voice barked, all humour gone as she ordered her two slaves to change. Obediently, they scuttled away in bowed silence.

Sardar gave me a nonchalant smile. 'Alana is the naughty one; we've got to watch her. Georgina is very submissive but always late. So naughty.' She held out a cigarette on a long black cigarette holder. She obviously expected me to light it for her.

I fumbled for a lighter.

'Oh, you're hopeless. There is a lighter over there.' She motioned impatiently, or perhaps she was simply practising before going 'on stage'. Was this the famous Method technique?

Her dominance was increasing; she began to strut back and forth. In a moment she was puffing away elegantly, her eyes no longer playful; she had become someone else to me. I kept my distance now.

'I'll probably just stub this out in their mouths for starters. I am in a devilish mood today. You'll see.'

A long cool stream of smoke billowed into my face. Everyone was becoming different somehow. Even I was thinking with a

**73**

director's hat on – my head was full of best shots, lighting, shadow, sound and mood. We had all gone into our own separate orbits but were soon to collide again. The atmosphere was not menacing but rather theatrical, with an undercurrent of unexpected danger. I got behind the camera; it was a barrier, a form of protection to shield me from the laughing dominatrix. The film world had become my personal comfort zone.

Alana and Georgina came back into the room, any sign that they were respectable men working in the City now gone. Their transformation was complete with PVC bras and shiny knickers, and Georgina added the fetching touch of wearing fishnets with suspenders. Both had black high heels on. Not to be outdone, Alana had on eyeliner, lipstick and coquettish cheap perfume. They still looked masculine but now they exuded confidence. Was their reassurance boosted by the barrier of clothing and makeup? Perhaps it was a crutch, like the camera was for me.

Things were moving quickly now.

'On your knees, slaves. Who wants to be the ashtray for me? Good girl, Alana.' Sardar flicked hot ash on to the tip of Alana's tongue and Alana swallowed gratefully.

A few puffs later, it was Georgina's turn as Sardar extinguished the cigarette in his mouth. The glowing cigarette butt was slowly ground into his tongue. I winced.

'Show everyone your servitude, Georgina. To camera, there's a good girl. Now say thank you.' Sardar smiled into the camera. 'What a good girl you are, Georgina. Ah, but Alana is getting jealous.' Sardar ground her stiletto boots into the side of the submissive transvestite.

Alana nearly cried out in pain but suppressed the urge.

'Lick my boots, you naughty girls.'

The pair obeyed instantly, licking the shiny boots up and down their length. It went on like this for some 20 minutes; some face slapping, kissing and licking the boots, the occasional cuff around the head, another cigarette, the occasional lash across the back with a six-tailed lash called a martinet, all of it lulling me into a false sense of security. Was *this* a Queening session?

My uninformed male opinion was brought crashing down in an instant. With the first sound of electrical crackling, my hairs stood on end. There was another, and I swung the camera in horror on to the glass wand in Sardar's hand. She smiled sweetly but the vibe had changed – the room had become charged, not so much with electricity as with raw, vicious intentions coupled with the expectations of the subs. Pain would be swift: the slaves tensed inwardly. Another electrical crackling signalled the regal opening of the matriarchal Queening session.

Sardar ripped down the PVC panties poor Georgina was wearing, sharply yanking his flaccid member upwards. She was clearly a practised mistress – she smiled, tormented, teased and cajoled, all the while stroking the wand on the hairs of Georgina's testes. Another sharp sound marked the singed hairs of his genitals. His body was arched in fear but his face told otherwise. Then came the first rub of excruciating agony. The scream was muffled as Georgina bit his lip.

My camera shot moved as I followed the activity, and it was then I noticed my own stomach muscles had tensed in sympathy. Or was it fear? My body seemed to have a mind of its own in mimicking the action of Georgina.

Again the wand moved in, but no, Sardar was just teasing. A bead of sweat formed on my brow but I couldn't wipe it away as both hands were operating the camera. A salty tear went into my left eye straight down from my brow. The dungeon had become close, an intimate domain of a vicious Goddess. Now for the first time I understood some of the residual energies I felt left behind in my abode in Brighton.

## Two's Company; Three's a Crowd

The session was buzzing, and I could see that Sardar was too, although she was carefully holding it back. By now Sardar was flaying the slaves' back with the martinet. The sounds went into red on the tiny camera's sound monitor on the cheap in-built camera mike, and I cursed that I had no external microphone. Although I imagine no one else would have cared, as the one-handed punters on the net are only interested in getting their rocks off. This video snippet was destined for Sardar's website so her other virtual slaves could get off. The Marquis de Sade would have been proud of me, I thought.

Grabbing Alana by the throat, Sardar spat in his face and threw him down to beg again. Georgina was made to grovel. After about 20 minutes, I thought the routine had become somewhat formulaic. Part of me relaxed, part of me was bored and part of me wondered why I had bothered turning up at all. I could have got this from a Nick Broomfield documentary and saved myself the effort of coming here to film.

Mistress Sardar cracked open a bottle of beer and drank its contents, bolting it back. The session became surreal as the slaves quietly licked her heels, as she sat on a low whipping bench joking with them. No longer in character, she too relaxed and conversation between them became natural; the role play had subsided. Alana kissed the sides of the boots and made his way upwards, only to be patted on the head with the handle of the leather lash and told to concentrate on the heels once more.

Georgina was rewarded for his obedience with a feather boa draped across his shoulders and allowed to kiss the Mistress's gloved hand, but only fleetingly. The hand teased and was whisked away.

Sardar stood up abruptly. 'Georgina, take your place face upwards under the Queening Throne. Come quickly.'

Georgina went on all fours to the appointed place face upwards, mouth opened in readiness.

'Alana, you naughty girl, sit next to him.'

Alana too scurried off obediently as prompted.

Sardar lifted the seat of the demonic Queening Throne to reveal that it was, in fact, a commode. A great gaping hole separated the seat from one underneath by some six inches. Sardar hoisted her skirt unceremoniously and pulled down her panties. Sitting down, she then gushed an unrelenting stream of urine into the open mouth of Georgina, who didn't flinch. The sound was identical to filling any other receptacle and you knew by the high-pitched sound that his mouth was soon full.

'Swallow the champagne, Georgina.'

He needed no further prompts, guzzling it down virtually in one before being treated to a refill. Now I could see why Sardar drank beer.

At this juncture, Freddy sidled in, his massive frame clad in a skin-tight black PVC tutu. My non-camera eye looked at him as the other tried in vain to follow the action. His massive shoulders stretched the material to breaking point, below which his thinner, ivory-white, hairy legs seemed out of place.

'I'm 'ere, Mistress.' The scene was about as sexy as filling in a tax return on a dreary Monday.

'Strip for the camera, Daniella.' Sardar looked distinctly unimpressed at the sight of her minder.

The two slaves dared to look up. I suppose in hindsight they wanted to enjoy this man's humiliation as much as anything. He was joining in their ordeal, after all.

I suddenly became aware of a certain fetid vinegar odour filling the air. It was then that my camera began jumping up and down beyond my control. I was completely at a loss to know why. Then the solid bolus of puke jammed in my throat. My mind disengaged from filming and I realised I was throwing up.

The smell was almost beyond description. Before my mind registered it, my body had already done so. Instinctively, I was already reacting to a stench that is encapsulated somewhere between the male genitals and the anus – in common terms, 'ball sweat'! – and the room was filled with it as Freddy stripped.

As much as I tried to suppress it, puke spilled down my top, but not before I had dropped the camera. For professionals reading this, I would like to say it was the only time in my life I have dropped a camera on the job – so to speak. I rushed to the toilet. Feelings of shame came over me as I had, in effect, abandoned the shoot. Fellow cameramen and directors will know that this is something no self-respecting professional would do – not even in a war zone. Better to rearrange the bodies of the dead than to leave a battlefield without a roll of good film. Something inside me was raging – I too had been pushed to extremity and had failed. I stuffed two pieces of toilet roll soaked in aftershave into my nostrils, pulled off the puke-stained top and rushed back into the dungeon. I picked up the camera which thankfully was still rolling and continued. No one had batted an eyelid as they were all engrossed in the Queening session.

Freddy was naked, facing the Queening trio. His facial expression was a constant blank canvas. It was as if the Mistress was the only one able to write upon it, and so she did. Her voice did actually seem to animate him. Now fully engorged, he was thrusting himself upon Alana and Georgina. By this time, he had thrust a huge dildo into himself that was constantly pointing dangerously near to me in the small room. I was feeling no less sick, albeit for different reasons now. My final impression of the Queening session was that it was something close to a private orgy, as it left the clearly defined precincts of a paid bondage session to give free rein to every sexual preference. Everyone seemed to get off at the Queening session. The vibes were very strange, ending with complete post-orgasmic calm for all involved. Peace had returned. I handed over the tapes and no one even said goodbye as I left.

## Babalon – Gateway to the Goddess

Minutes after this session, while carrying my equipment away, my mouth still rancid from puke and my mind numbed by what I had seen, and more to the point smelled, I felt myself start to have a sort of psychic experience.

Although I am not a cynic, when I hear of people channelling entities it always seems to me that many are based on wishful thinking – for example, the 'regression to Atlantis' scenario, with the exception of Edgar Casey. Why is it that these people always seem to channel things like crystal light bearers from Atlantis or the High Priestess of Lemuria shrouded in white light? Whatever happened to the lowly toilet cleaners of the antediluvian kingdom or the poor nurses cleaning up the sick and urine of their senile Atlantean charges? There are also a long line of self-congratulating would-be psychics claiming to have been a Native American chief among the high plains, or a Mayan guardian of the pyramids in the jungle or an Indian saint practising yoga. There have unquestionably been genuine cases of the above, but they are few and far between. I have come to the conclusion that, for the gullible, these dubious regressive states offer a brain function somewhere between dreaming and fantasy. It must be very reassuring to imagine that you have been a major player in some myth or major historical event, but it seems to have little to do with the real world of the here and now.

Now, having said all of the above, and bearing in mind that I have sought out and questioned some of those individuals who make such claims, I still believe something of this kind happened to me along the busy Pentonville Road – close to Angel underground station in north London, just after the Queening session. Pentonville Road is not the most esoteric location in London; it is one of the busiest in the area, connecting Euston, King's Cross and St Pancras to both the north and west of the city, and it is populated by beggars, junkies and their taciturn dealers. It is far from idyllic, certainly not the obvious setting for something out-of-the-ordinary, but here it was that I began receiving some sort of inner signal that directly pertains to the thread in this book. The dreamlike message came from nowhere and left me wondering whether I was actually drawing certain forces towards me, like a magnet does iron filings, or had I just joined the ranks of the woolly navel gazers? Or, worse still, had I become yet another crank, a mildly schizophrenic denizen of modern London?

I felt the inner B-movie actor within me rebel. I cynically stubbed out a cigarette in disgust and removed to a safe distance in order to pour scorn on it all – but to no avail. I was taken aback that I had had this experience. It was a bit scary, to say the least, not in a horrific way, but deep inside myself, as my own beliefs were challenged – but by whom? Could I trust such an experience? Was it madness or self-deception? The latter cannot be written off too readily.

Travelling east, I passed by the mound just off Pentonville Road, surrounded by high Victorian iron railings. Standing little more than 20ft high, it houses nothing more spectacular than a reservoir station pumping water. My body shuddered and I stepped into a self-contained bubble of space and time. Everything stopped. All city sounds ceased, my thoughts were suspended. Over and over, the word Babalon came to my mind without meaning or purpose. Each time, Babalon became louder as if to emphasise the first calling. The bubble burst and the sounds of the 21st century came rushing in with great gusto. I walked on mechanically, wondering what had just happened to me. By the time I came to, I was at Penton Church; clearly I had wandered completely off course in a daze.

Nearly two years later, I discovered that Penton Reservoir, where this happened, is in fact the very spot that once contained a stone circle said to be a Druidic ritual site. The word Babalon means gateway to the Goddess.

I don't attach any significance or try to explain the experience, but mention it in passing as it was bizarre and as odd as anything that had occurred at Sardar's place. Nothing like that has happened to me since.

Back in Brighton, I felt as if the bondage dungeon had taken on yet another countenance. I began to recognise the energy that was inside the room. A residual presence of Sardar-like impressions was seeping out, and I began to believe that places do not change, thoughts remain. Sometimes, the emanations from places are so strong that nothing seems to wipe their traces, as if an idea or an activity reaches a certain frequency and can never be switched off again. That place is marked and must repeat its fate over and over. I was convinced that the bondage dungeon in Brighton began to attract dark erotic forces, but it also seemed to be aiding me in some way. Perhaps this is how people begin to go mad and I actually thought that for a while. As at the start of a new love affair, I began to see less of the outside world and more of the sinister bondage dungeon. Ever mindful of climbing the ceilings of my mind, an internal psychogeographical map of erotic ramblings began to unfold.

As I had resigned as a model agent for the girls, I now had time on my hands and I began writing feverishly in the bondage dungeon, which had become my new office.

Soon after, I received an interesting call from a proper pornographer of the old school, who wanted to pick my brains on digital magazine distribution. He had been given my details by a Brighton journalist, who knew I was writing a book and offered to help, if he could. Serendipity perhaps?

Within hours I was on my way to a very unusual meeting indeed.

# CHAPTER 4

# FUCK THE CUSTOMER; FUCK THE SUPPLIER

## *The Good Old Days*

'Fuck the customer; fuck the supplier.' These were the very first words uttered to me by a man whom we shall call Tony, a former clip-joint owner in London's Soho, whom I first met at a Thai restaurant to discuss distribution rights in Holland. It transpired that he owned the rights to several old titles. Tony, a British citizen of Maltese extraction, is now approaching his 70th year, but he ran his racket in Soho's notorious heyday during the 1960s and 70s and spent four decades building a small porn empire, a venture that began with a shop containing film booths in London's Soho, leading to a clip joint – a drinking club where customers were lured in to watch dancers or strippers but then were presented with a hefty bill for drinks, and were unable to leave until they had parted with the cash. Later he dabbled in sex shops both licensed and unlicensed, the latter being the type that are regularly raided and shut down by police. He retired from Soho in 1982. In later years he branched out into the property boom, using the equity to fund much greater enterprises in film and entertainment, design studios and no doubt other more nefarious rackets. The spoils must have been good, as he owns several houses in the UK, Malta and elsewhere, but Tony was always modest and above all a realist.

'You see, it didn't matter in them days if you swept the floor or not, a punter would come in and spend money; as for the suppliers, if they didn't do deals with us, well we just fucked them all the time. Sex-shop owners didn't give a flying but now it's different. Soho is not what it used to be. Soho is finished. The council have handed over the powers to the police. It means that the raids will come again. People will get nicked. More shops closed down,' he lamented.

Tony was not a fast eater, enjoying the food and the lager equally. He surveyed the bar carefully, weighing up every customer before going on as if he was being observed. 'I am genuinely gutted about Soho going down the pan; we've had our laughs. Years ago, when I ran the booths, I remember I was young and full of bravado. Ha. The police came round raiding us on a Friday to cause as much disruption as possible. They would collect the semen-stained tissues off the floor of each cubicle as evidence. I would 'ave a go – "Look, lads, the cleaners are in again." I right pissed them off.' He sipped his lager thoughtfully. 'In them days it was Paul Raymond and the Maltese who ran the whole show. There were a few other Jewish guys hustling for a piece like Bernie Silver – he ran the whole show for a while. Everyone was gents in them days – well, they still are, but the government doesn't want you to earn a crust, do they? Robbing bastards. They sell arms all round the world, prop up dictatorships, put council tax on the poor and then tell me porn is wrong. It's mad, innit?'

Later the conversation turned to police involvement in the porn trade in Soho. 'The Old Bill in those days were all right as long as you kept close to someone, say, of the rank of chief superintendent. They would basically warn everyone that the hunting season was about to begin: "Don't take the piss." If you were still doing naughty things and the hunting season began, well, you only had yourself to blame. There is a difference between pornography and prostitution and there are some things the Old Bill will never tolerate. Once the Old Bill know you, say they felt your collar a couple of times, you're like an old friend, they come up and talk to you, maybe have a meal and a chat, even a game of squash is not out of the question.' Tony was staring at me intently.

'How friendly is friendly?' It was not a naive question, nor indiscreet.

'It depends how deep you are in, or how deep they *think* you are in. Some people used to give the Old Bill a drink to keep 'em sweet, but that can work both ways because now you have committed another crime and a serious one, plus you've got this guy breathing down your neck, sniffing around for more. If you piss him off it is another loose cannon waiting in the wings. You can actually find yourself working for the Old Bill, instead of the Old Bill working for you, and he'll want info against other firms; then it is dangerous. The best policy is not to pay the Old Bill but to outwit him.'

Tony did not seem about to expand any further but I could not resist one more question. 'But if you are taking them out for squash, golf or whatever it must be hard not to get too involved in, say, paying for drinks and ending up getting too close?'

'Put it this way. If the Old Bill know who you are and what you do and you're the kind of guy who listens, you don't take the piss, you are on the good side morally, when things are getting hot, you play the game and clean up, go with the flow – you've already won half the battle. If you get nicked, and you will in Soho, you've got to take it on the chin like a gent, don't take it personally, it's business. Old Bill know you are not going away because it's your livelihood, so it is easier to work with you a bit than against you. I mean, in those days we handed them paedophiles and we have always played the game on violent prostitution rackets, forced sex slaves and the like, and the Old Bill needed our co-operation. So that is one way, if you like, how we used to pay them off. There were some, of course, who literally passed round the hat to all and sundry, but then the whole house of cards collapses around your ears. But then they were the governors of Soho.' Tony shrugged. 'Like I say, in the old days, it depended how deeply you wanted to get involved.'

# FUCK THE CUSTOMER; FUCK THE SUPPLIER

Whether this was an invitation or a cue for me to shut up I didn't quite know, but at this point I felt my curiosity had taken me to the brink of knowledge that could later undo me. To be honest, I did not have the courage to ask how deeply Tony was once involved. It was time to enjoy the Thai meal.

## Soho: A Fistful of Dollars

Some weeks later, Tony's words echoed through my mind as police began to target Soho once more. There was a crackdown on unlicensed sex shops, those who traded without parting with the necessary £30,000 a year for a council licence. One of the best ways to close such a rogue trader is to find something on the premises that contravenes the Obscene Publications Act. The Act is to some degree a catch-all offence that allows the police a certain amount of discretion as to what is obscene and corrupting to moral standards within a person's mind; for example, the portrayal of the snorting of cocaine contravenes the Act, but I don't see copies of Al Pacino's *Scarface* being seized. Of course, these laws were mostly formulated and passed in the 19th century, although a raft of modern amendments appeared in the late 50s and are, to say the least, outdated or outmoded. They decree what you and I may or may not view, or even produce. We must understand that many Victorian laws have remained on the statute books, and whether they are enforced or not can depend on an officer's own prejudices.

In the heart of Soho, in a small Victorian passageway, there remains a cluster of unlicensed shops plying their trade. These premises cater for some specialist material such as fetish and gay and lesbian, among other more mainstream titles. By comparison, the more enlightened parts of Europe would view these shops as very mild, almost vanilla in taste and not at all shocking or extreme. But in the UK they have been targeted by police and raided, with vendors arrested, DNA'ed, photographed, fingerprinted and maybe even charged, if the Crown Prosecution Service thinks the evidence is sufficient.

One fateful day in Soho, a police raid was mounted on an unlicensed sex shop with several offending discs being seized. To the horror of arresting officers, a white American girl appeared in a Czech film featuring a Stalinist-type fantasy. British Police wasted no time in handcuffing the shop owner and frogmarching him out of the shop for further questioning. He was subsequently charged with possession of the disc under the Obscene Publications Act and bailed to appear before magistrates.

Having feared that the film featured some form of modern slavery, the police subsequently discovered that the American model had willingly starred in this film, which showed her being beaten severely by her tormentors.

As an ironic aside, while the raid was in progress, only two Soho streets away the American actress was in a council-licensed sex shop openly signing copies of the very same film for her fans. She has, in fact, appeared in several of their productions, becoming one of the Czech studio's biggest assets.

## FUCK THE CUSTOMER; FUCK THE SUPPLIER

She has now also added a published book to her credits, in which she states her enjoyment of making these types of films. Her Soho video signing was a highly publicised event, which one suspects must have reached the ears of someone in officialdom. Why were these discs deemed illegal in one shop and not in another? Why was a star of the banned film allowed to parade these wares in public only a few streets away as another shop owner was led away to the cells? When the actress heard of the farcical arrest, she was incensed by such arbitrary justice and vowed to appear in court to defend the arrested man and challenge the outdated obscenity law.

However, considering his rather precarious position, along with its jail implications, the defendant chose to plead guilty, leading well away from a high-profile trial with a vociferous actress condemning archaic laws. His guilty plea, while shaving a considerable slice off the jail sentence, prevented the news of such double standards reaching the ears of the taxpayer. He was duly sentenced to three months' imprisonment and removed to Brixton Jail.

As each case unfolds, one can only wonder if such a catch-all law might lead some shop owners to throw themselves at the mercy of corrupt officials in order to trade. Tony's comments were echoed by many in the Soho sex trade.

In my opinion, Soho is always going to be a breeding ground for such knavery, due to the porn trade being driven partly underground, which inevitably causes social problems.

**91**

In times past, the tricks used in unlicensed sex shops were less than sophisticated. A punter would enter the shop and ask for a VHS video of a certain film and, to avoid saying he didn't have it in stock, the vendor would go out the back. Some time later, he would produce the VHS tape complete with a label displaying the required title and sell it to the unsuspecting victim, who by the time he got home would find he had bought something completely different – usually the old stock that needed shifting. This trick was not as bad as some who simply gave out blank tapes. A more daring trick involved the vendor, standing in front of the counter, entering into conversation with the punter. If the punter said he was visiting London and it was clear he was not a local man or regular customer, the vendor would step behind the counter and take the money for the goods but, before handing them over, he would say he just had to go next door to get some more carrier bags. Two minutes later, another man would enter the shop from the back room pretending to be the real vendor, who, feigning surprise and dismissing the first seller as a fraud, would tell the punter he had been ripped off. The shopper had lost his money but few would report the fraud for obvious reasons.

There were as many scams as there were punters, all increasing in sophistication as time went on. One favourite scam of the more unscrupulous unlicensed sex-shop owner was selling data records of customers where possible to bigger firms, and, although not strictly illegal, such records were another source of revenue. Customers would receive spam and unsolicited mail advertising various seedy products, which could prove to be very embarrassing if a wife or a girlfriend opened the mail to see the words 'Dear Valued Customer'. Any anonymity was blown out of the water. Credit-card fraud was a popular scam perpetrated by unlicensed merchants, particularly if a shop expected to be closed down within six months, although operators who conducted this type of activity would definitely feel the heat when they reopened elsewhere. This was considered by almost everyone as 'taking the piss', to quote Tony.

The subterfuge within the unlicensed shops themselves had to be seen to be believed. As the situation now stands, the 'real' owners of these premises are twice removed and are never arrested, relying on the workers in the shops to take responsibility when raids take place. Therefore, the vendors of these unregulated premises are to some degree always ready for their eventual brush with the law. More experienced vendors join an illicit shop for the first few months then bail out before trouble knocks, although this safety formula doesn't always work, as police can strike at any moment. This has led to a peculiar mentality where everyone is after a dollar at every opportunity, come what may; as such, there is little loyalty or sentimentality in the trade. If the 'real' untouchable owner is none the wiser, special pirate goods will be brought in on certain lines by the shop workers themselves, who will sell these for cash without declaring to any other staff that such sales have been made. The 'real' owner is therefore being booted internally by his own organisation with under-the-counter sales. It is a common problem in this illicit trade.

It has led to the rise in importance of the distributors, who have become the trusted lieutenants of the owners, as the last thing anyone wanted was for the counter staff to have a piece of the action. I finally understood Tony's first comments to me and realised that, in such a world, it could not be any other way.

### The Trusted Lieutenant

In the pyramid structure of the unlicensed porn shops in Soho, it is clear to see that a hierarchy exists. First and foremost, there must be the financial principal behind the shop or shops, then naturally there must be a factory supplying the goods to the shops, which may also include some pirated wares. On the second rung of the ladder, there is a distributor who visits and stocks the shop(s); this may involve several distributors but only one in practice who supplies the pirated goods. Next in an ideal scenario is a trusted employee who manages the shop with temporary staff on cash wages.

If the financial principal is also producing products for other outlets, then his distributor must become his trusted lieutenant; this is crucial, otherwise his revenue will be severely depleted. At every shop, the lieutenant should be able to look and see what products are being sold, what is popular and worth pirating, see how many copies are on shelves, check sales quickly and gauge if internal piracy is at work. Any other rival pirates he identifies must be closed down in the network through contra deals, even threats of cutting off supplies of good saleable products. It is a cut-throat business, but the lieutenant is key to ensuring that the principal's products are paramount in everyone's mind.

The distributor who works outside of the principal's control must also be brought into the fold by financial reward and inducement. Booted products can be given to this type of distributor free of charge, but with the caveat, 'Push our products over all others.' Some of these distributors cover the length and breadth of Britain and their eyes and ears are literally worth hundreds of thousands of pounds in revenue. A small fleet of anonymous white vans traverse the motorways and byways of Britain ferrying their precious cargos; these independent traders are the lifeblood of the product-based porn trade. God forbid they should ever crash and spill their wares upon the streets.

As a filmmaker myself, I was quite alarmed at the scale and complexity of the duplicity involved in the porn trade, and, as a film distributor, Tony's comments alarmed me – was piracy as rife as he seemed to suggest? Tony knew I wanted to write a book for which I needed to draw upon interesting experiences, plus he knew I required money to do this. It seemed natural that he should introduce me into the eco-chain as I would be very useful, or so he thought, to his future secret internet plans. At the time, I was unaware of this, but Tony had agreed to help me anyway, so I stopped worrying.

## Blood Brothers

After the meeting with Tony, I wandered about Soho where I met separately at least three Albanians I had known from Brighton. They were very friendly and greeted me as an old friend. One was working as a waiter by day and doorman by night, having gained his registered SIA security badge; another was shady about his income, but I strongly suspected he was involved in the red-light business somewhere down the line; and the third, Artaan, was unashamedly working with the clan-based Albanian Mafia – in a chapter calling themselves the Prostinetta Alliance (I translate roughly through Italian from Albanian). I suspected that the name was a joke. It reminded me of the 17th-century criminal fraternities of London – described by author Fergus Linnane in his book *London Crime and Vice* – whereby money was raised by the group to pay good defence lawyers or to be dispensed to someone upon their release from jail. Interest-free loans were also available from the Alliance to start new schemes.

After a mammoth drinking session in Soho with Artaan, we became blood brothers. His attitude was that the Albanians were the up-and-coming force in Soho, but, although I did not want to contradict that comment, it was clear to me that they were following a well-beaten path already trodden by the Maltese some 50 years earlier. The Albanians were the sharp end of the rackets but owned next to nothing in property, goods or services. That was still the preserve of the English, Jews and Maltese, whose invisible hands moved everything along. The blood pact in itself provided me with the support of the group, but also meant that I could be called upon to kill or maim anyone who harmed him or vice versa. From my point of view, it also meant that we would meet in another lifetime. Artaan and I exchanged telephone numbers.

## The Call of the Wild

Making films and videos is one thing but distribution is an altogether different ballgame. It is an art with strategies as convoluted as chess but governed by the rules of logic. Keep the rights long after people have forgotten the films, and new opportunities always arise. Create a brand on the back of a film or, better still, take your product to the net. Filmmaking, particularly since the advent of the cheap but efficient video camera, is an open invitation for every peeping Tom, Dick and Harry to make an adult flick. Couple this with the Web 2 technology of YouTube, Flickr and various adult promotional sites, and who needs filmmakers? But you will need a good distributor if you become serious about what you do.

Tony vouched for me as a distributor. It was dangerous to go it alone now and I was increasingly aware that I needed support and introductions – references, if you like – in order to penetrate this darkly secretive world. The people involved were very generous both with time and contacts; they wanted to do business and all acts were in good faith. Unless you knocked them for money or pirated their goods, all was well. Even shortfalls in payments or products could be discussed as long as you were straight. It was definitely a very civilised, gentlemanly affair but there was no doubt that, if someone were ever to take this as a sign of weakness, they would be sorely mistaken. Soho was built on its own unique code of honour.

I was becoming torn between my loyalty to these people and writing my book. Had it influenced me to such a degree that everything was now too entwined and I was losing my direction? Had I in some way been bought off? These questions were circling my head when a mysterious package arrived, delivered by two men dressed in suits and dark glasses. Immediately, I thought someone was pulling my leg, until I received an anonymous call from Tony – caller withheld. He was acting very mysteriously.

'Open the package. Inside is £5K for you. Get a ticket to Amsterdam. The address is in there. Don't read it out on the phone. See the man, set up a business account with Kamer van Koophandel [Chamber of Commerce]. Ask about credit-card processing for the web with a bank. ING are good but any bank will do. Bring back any discs the bloke offers you. Keep the change. Come back as suggested. Don't try to bring back anything else interesting. See me when you're back.'

Tony hung up. I realised for the first time that he was certainly not retired; it seemed Soho was run by the old boys, not the burly young guys you see standing in strip-club doorways.

I get bored on holiday but I love foreign travel, although Amsterdam is definitely not my favourite city and I was not too thrilled at the prospect of a visit there. It is flat, the weather is worse than England, and the canals are a pain to navigate, especially when the bridge is drawn up. Dutch cuisine – well, it's not right, is it? If I want to smoke dope, I can smoke it anywhere in the UK. It is not really an issue. As for Dutch beer, it gives more head than half the girls working the 'Dam.

But I was intrigued. Tony's cloak-and-dagger routine had somehow managed to make what was probably going to be a very boring trip suddenly really exciting.

I had used all the right safeguards. But could I trust him?

# Chapter 5

# A MAID MAN

## *Flatlanders*

Arriving at Shipol airport is a pleasure. Customs are cool if you are travelling from the UK. Because they are not fighting any foreign wars, even terrorism is at a bit of a blue-alert level. No stop and search in the Netherlands – land of the free.

Upon arrival, I had forgotten my misgivings about the trip; there was a buzz in the air and, once back in Amsterdam, I realised that the place does have its charms after all. But I draw the line at the cuisine. Yes, there are some great restaurants in the city but they are generally French. Coffee shops smell of the pungent, expansive aroma of states of mind, belonging to a number of potential realities. Amsterdam encourages that outlook. This time around I copped an executive attitude about it. Come and go, take the cash, discs, whatever else, and leave. I intended to check out the transvestites if time allowed, but this was business. Leave all coffee shops alone until safely away from other people's money.

Although my passport was not moody, I was travelling under the alias 'Donovan'. I had once done some business between two conflicting countries, involving a currency to gold exchange, and had to change my name by deed poll in order to complete the deal. So now Mr Donovan kind of fitted in with the 'Dam feel. I bumped into a few people I knew but generally kept a low profile during my stay. The only touristy thing I did was visit the Erotic Museum in oz achterburgwal, its five floors of erotica showing just about everything, as curious couples floated around and a few seedy raincoat types shuffled about. I would describe it as a modern equivalent of the penny arcade machines called 'What the Butler Saw', once popular in all good British seaside resorts. After putting a penny into the machine, you cranked a handle and looked through a viewing hood, where behind a glass screen there was a series of peepshow photographs that worked like a flipbook. The photographs were flicked through the action of the crank handle, so you could go through the sequences fast or slow but never halt on a particular picture. The mechanism was designed so that it went backwards when this happened, with no chance of extending your peepshow that way. I first saw one when I was seven or eight, and unsupervised, I must add.

Leaving the Erotic Museum, I felt a bit of an anorak – it is one of those places you ought to visit as a couple really.

But although I believed myself not easily shocked, what was on display in the museum could not begin to compare with what I would see at the meeting Tony had arranged. In fact it was enough to make a seasoned customs officer flinch, leaving me feeling slightly uncomfortable with pornography. I was pushing my own boundaries. I know that these limits are set in all of us, some natural, some nurtured. Much of our sexuality may be natural as a consequence of genetic codes, but a lot of it is based on early experiences and, to a degree, accidental conditioning. Until I visited the porn warehouse, I had actually been completely innocent in my eddying whirlpools of thought. I was about to move onto an altogether different scale of experience that would change my views forever.

## In the Belly of the Beast

I had made up my mind to make the best of the trip, and I was enjoying the break as I headed out of town to the main appointment.

The gentle grey road with a steep grassy bank had idling, languid canals at either side. A well-trodden footpath on one side ended at the bridge, where a T-junction pointed the traveller towards various places with outlandish names. It was sunny and all around seemed innocent and orderly. I felt invigorated, walking briskly without the aid of either map or GPS.

Finally, the journey was over and I stood before a solitary building in the flat countryside. It was like a steel sardine can consisting of what seemed to be two floors, which turned out to be a very deceptively large warehouse. I entered the security gate, gave my ID and waited. A buzz back from security allowed me to proceed across a tarmaced car park to the reception. Outside, two rather starched corporate blondes holding files were chatting. I could have been at the headquarters of any number of large corporations, as the outward demeanour was entirely mercantile, almost industrial in style, with no hint of what was inside. Even the signage was discreet, and the whole area was bordered by sterile manicured gardens.

I passed through a smoked-glass door making my way across to a lithe, pretty girl of about 25, another blonde, sitting at a desk busily typing on a small laptop. She looked up and beamed. I told her I had an appointment with Tony's contact, and she replied in perfect English, 'Good morning. Please take a seat. Would you like a coffee while you wait?'

A few moments later, she handed over the cup with a smile and returned to her busy schedule, every inch the corporate employee.

Harry, as we shall call him, walked into the reception foyer. He was over six foot six, wiry, tanned and with a very healthy physique; I took him to be in his early forties, but later he revealed he was over fifty. He spoke fluent English and exuded charm and physical vitality in equal measure, his pumping handshake reinforcing the impression that he kept himself in good shape.

After entering his office, we sat either side of a large pine desk. Harry had been in the Dutch armed forces in his younger years, before leaving to volunteer to photograph dolphins and killer whales off the coast of Iceland. He had a lifelong interest in marine life, and his hobby was photographing and cataloguing fishing stocks to study the ecology of the creatures. Subsequently, this interest in photography led him into another area of life, and by the 1980s he had opened his first porn business.

I came to realise as he spoke that this was the man Tony had warned me about when we had our Thai meal. 'He is Dutch – ex-special forces. Anyone boots him gets their heads kicked in. Full stop. You have to know when to pirate and when not to.'

Harry was also keen on kickboxing and personal fitness training. We talked about the martial-arts movie business in Malaysia for a while, but then the time came for me to find out what the hell was going on. Why was I here? The preamble had been pleasant enough but my curiosity had been triggered to the point where I wanted to be let off the hook, and to take the inevitable cash rewards.

'I understand you have registered the address with the Kamer van Koophandel, right? And opened the bank account for transfer of funds?'

I nodded.

'OK, great. I will transfer 30,000 euros in there for you tomorrow, unless you require another currency, of course. No? That's fine. I am going to give you some new products that we have ready for launch on the market. Choose your titles and feel free to copy those you wish to vend in London; we only need a reciprocal title in the same genre. The products must be on the shelf, fully packaged, within five days. The Germans will pirate everything within three to four weeks, so it is very important that we act in unison.'

'The Germans? How do they come into it?' I blurted out.

'The German business model is not one of a team player. They are the worst pirates in Europe and taking a large slice of business away. The idea we have between Holland and Soho is to release in unison on certain titles with fast distribution. In fact, most of these titles are themselves taken from the websites of the Germans and downloaded on to DVD. They make good porn.'

'So the Germans are not pirating this stuff, we are pirating them?' It was a trite observation but I waited for the answer.

Harry laughed. 'Let's just say the tide has turned,' he said, handing me a DVD.

I looked in horror as it was an animal-porn title, with a very graphic front cover.

'It is actually German but we have altered the cover to make it look as if it is from the Netherlands. Once the punter sees it, does he care that it is in German, after all? Can he report such a thing as false advertising?' Again Harry laughed.

'Well, no, this is illegal, Harry, and if you think I am taking that back to the UK you've got another thing coming.' I was absolutely appalled, hardly wanting to touch the box as I recoiled from it. It completely freaked me out. I felt dirty, bemused, shocked and angry all at once.

## A MAID MAN

'Come, Jon, I will show you the warehouse.' Harry was laughing at my face, which no doubt looked disgusted at his suggestion.

When he stood up, I noticed he looked older than I had first thought, but still rippled with muscle; he patted me on the back and nearly took my breath away. I followed him out into the warehouse.

Down along a blank magnolia corridor, through two or three spring-loaded doors, we were soon inside the warehouse, which was much larger than it seemed on the outside – a veritable tardis of sexual fantasy of all genres lay ahead. It seemed there was something for everyone in here, enough to surprise even the most jaded of erotic adventurers. I considered myself privileged to be here and realised that Tony had granted it as a favour – at least I took it that way. I was being given the red-carpet treatment and knew instinctively that it was nothing to do with me or my mission. Or at least not entirely.

Forklift trucks beeped their horns as they careered around corners at high speed, holding pallets of DVDs or going to pick one up. Row upon row of cellophane-wrapped pallets were piled high in numbered box units. Aisle after aisle of porn was ready to be shipped out around the world. I must admit I was humbled by the sheer scale of this place and its contents. Workers wore dark blue and busied themselves, never once looking around; this was a hub of commercial success where even the nature of the product was immaterial – it could just as easily have been baked beans. When you arrive at this magnitude of product, even the old pornographers' adage, 'Content is king,' is no longer wholly appropriate and pales into insignificance. Here content of any kind did not matter. Uber-Porn Central had arrived.

Harry handled me in his cool style, neither becoming larger than life nor patronising me. He watched as I took in the sight of the warehouse. 'We must wear hi-viz jackets if we are in here,' he said, handing me a yellow jerkin stitched with reflective side stripes.

I put it on as Harry made a call in Dutch on an internal phone and, within half a minute, a dark-haired man in his early thirties called Marcel joined us. He was muscular but noticeably shorter than Harry, although I found it difficult to pay him any real attention as row upon row, level upon level of porn pallets overshadowed all other considerations – how much was this lot worth? It must have been billions of pounds, let alone dollars.

The tour began. I had imagined it would be broken down into genres or something but it was not that simple. There was a complex warehousing system based on most likely picking and packing. It didn't really sink in and the words washed over me as I remained fascinated by the sheer size and scale of the operation. We drifted past warehouse staff who smiled or nodded at Harry, then busied themselves in reading picking lists. Had we reached the corporate notion of porn – a perfect world where nothing was ruffled, where a super-efficient mercantile state had been achieved?

'How much is this lot worth?' I asked, unable to contain my curiosity.

'Not much. It is a commodity based on demand of the customer base. In reality it is just content-based value with no material asset. Come on, these are just discs with printed covers,' Harry answered in his perfect English.

'So, the real value of porn is content?' I was trying hard to understand and looked at Harry searchingly.

He shrugged and looked down at me. 'If DVD piracy continues to supply, then this warehouse of discs is worth nothing at all. The content has a value, which is why we protect copyright and hold that as the real value of the products. There was a situation after the collapse of communism where the Russians wanted to flood the market with artificial diamonds. If they had done this then the value of real diamonds would have fallen. The German government and the De Beers diamond corporation prevented the situation, by loaning the Russian government US$57 billion.'

Marcel continued as if scripted. 'In any market, diamonds or the DVDs in this workplace have always a perceived value held by supply and demand. In reality the real worth of diamonds, oil or DVDs are how much they cost to bring to your door. We are maintaining the current market value. We are saying to you that what the current value is, is what the customers will pay from their money. That is our business.' Marcel looked at Harry, who nodded in agreement.

Looking around, we came across a stray pallet in the middle of an aisle. Marcel and Harry looked at it, then carefully peeled back some cellophane wrapping holding the stacks of DVDs in place, which were also encased in a thicker plastic to keep them in neatly bundled stacks. A few loose titles were on top along with a printed list. This time it was granny porn.

We moved on again.

Throughout the tour we passed so many niches of pornography, each holding a different world view on sexuality, some strange, others more obvious – slut wives, amateur girls, cheerleaders, barely legal teens, ebony, live cams, Latino, MILF (Mothers I'd Like to Fuck), interracial, pantyhose, ugly, voyeur, dogging, Asian celebrity, female domination, big butts, bareback boys, drunk girls, pregnant porn, group sex orgies, foot worship, bondage, anal intercourse, rubber- and PVC-clad models, watersports, shaven women, non-nude, hirsute, Japanese Hentai, sex in public, she-males, BBW (big-breasted women) and so on. (Of course, I cannot mention all the cross-genres, sub-genres and micro-niches of each subject – for example, black orgy in public or shaven lesbians performing foot worship.)

'So many genres, so little time,' was my only observation. I compared it to the Great Library of Alexandria but dedicated to the human libido, and both Harry and Marcel laughed. Harry remarked that he hoped this one didn't get burned down by the authorities.

We returned to the office but not before passing a section of gonzo porn, where I stopped and questioned them. It turned out the term gonzo in porn meant exactly the same as in journalism, where the reporter is part of the scene themselves, but in this case it is the cameraman. The gonzo director was an American named Seymore Butts. I took a copy for research purposes.

## Bonfire of the Pirates

In the beginning there was 16mm piracy, which was very difficult to get into unless you owned or worked in a duplication house. Later, with the advent of video tape, video piracy became more accessible but you still needed to distribute to make it effective. Unless you owned a shop or were a crooked distributor with a shop owner on-side, piracy was not that lucrative and also fairly obvious. Then came the DVD. Digital content could be burned directly from DVD to DVD, or sent across the internet to other locations, hidden in members' areas on websites. Suddenly, those who had long enjoyed the spoils of piracy began to see the whole market share being gradually eroded in an unstoppable tide of bootleg copies. Home users, file sharers, bit torrents had all cut into the market. Producers could no longer justify making expensive productions as the return revenue had disappeared. Distributors could no longer compete with the worldwide web, and shop owners were competing with a myriad of cheap sites where customers could either buy direct or join a members' pay site and see a hundred such productions for the price of one.

It seemed Harry and Marcel, like Tony, wanted out. They had seen the writing on the wall – DVD was already a thing of the past. But what then was the future?

'If you really want to understand the future you must take one step beyond the private members' website where you are paying to see content. This idea has existed for over a decade and has proved very successful for people like *Playboy* and other producers. What we have seen and are interested in as major distributors in Europe is something called IPTV or internet television. That market is the future,' Harry told me. 'IPTV has something known as a content management system that protects copyright and helps prevent piracy. Using IPTV, it is possible to trace those copying your content and prosecute them. Hollywood is just beginning to look at this. From the porn point of view we can distribute en masse through this portal.' Harry looked directly at me.

So far I had managed to follow Harry's drift because I had been in the video business a long time. I knew that Hollywood didn't want to follow their cousins in the music industry, who had been decimated by the internet people like Napster. Hollywood had been searching for a way to fight piracy and file sharing.

It seemed Harry was on top of this issue. 'IPTV is streamed at high-definition video standard with no loss in quality, so the end user can view at real time anything he wants. We can archive that video stream or run it live or even run multiple screenings. This is where we have to go to survive.'

Tony's words came back to me: 'A video pirate today is a password trader tomorrow.' He had already told me where he was going. But this was very ambitious.

Marcel chipped in. 'We understand you trained with the

# A MAID MAN

Monty Python film school Panico in London, is that correct? You have been trained in television production management also?'

I nodded.

'It could be an interesting place for someone like you, don't you think?'

I was beginning to see why I had been brought here now. It seemed Tony was a very astute businessman.

'Our neighbours the Germans have already set up one IPTV channel that is very good. We are going to show you Dorcel TV. Study this. It is the future of porn.' Marcel picked up a remote control and turned on a TV, obviously rigged to a computer or set-top box, and it began to bring up a pink and mauve website – Dorcel TV, founded by Frenchman Marc Dorcel, which offered several different genres of porn.

'It is awash with new possibilities,' I said after a few minutes.

Harry gave me a stack of German DVDs. There was nothing illegal among them – the UK was pretty grey on some things but it was important to steer clear of blood, excrement, torture, rape, bestiality and, of course, the universal no-no of child porn.

'These will be ripped on to a hard drive. We strongly suggest you carry them on your person rather than inside your hand luggage. Return by boat as a foot passenger. I am sure you can do the rest. The hard drive will be dropped to your hotel this evening at 7 p.m.'

'Why don't you just FTP it across the net? It's a lot cheaper,' I asked, a common-sense question.

'FTP, like all digital footprints, is traceable; this hard-drive material is untraceable. Like this we are safe but everyone will know, of course. What you are doing is not illegal so don't worry. It was good meeting you.' Harry stood up, signalling the end of my tour.

Marcel smiled and led me out. 'There is a USB port in the hard drive so you can inspect everything before you leave. It will all be legal to possess in your country. As for copyrights …' Marcel let the sentence trail off.

We shook hands and I left to return to my hotel in Amsterdam. Here we were, 30 years down the line, still obeying the old adage, 'Fuck the supplier' – Tony was right.

## The Singapore Sweat

The hard drive was delivered exactly on time and I took it in the foyer from the inconspicuous delivery driver. Back in my room I hooked it up and inspected the German porn, which was all leather and lace – very innocuous by any standard. I wondered why all the drama was necessary. It didn't matter; I was going out to party that evening and had made up my mind to meet with two London contacts who were taking me to a transvestite club. I showered, changed and put on my duty-free aftershave. It smelled like fly spray and I wondered if somehow that was a counterfeit product as well – after all, one of the side effects of being in close proximity to pornographers over a certain period of time is that everything is viewed as a potential scheme. Any deviation from the norm and alarm bells start ringing. Your mind begins to suspect that someone, somewhere, is being rinsed of cash, contacts, product or some benefit to the advantage of the bigger fish. I was extremely concerned by my growing cynicism and tried to counter it by a healthy optimism. By doing so I became a cynical optimist.

Perhaps readers will expect me to have stashed the hard drive really well, maybe inside a grille of the air-con or heating system, or just above the suspended ceiling tile of the room, just in case. Well, I have already been there when I was in Singapore, staying at the RLCA on the top floor. I was asked to stash a million US dollars, when the dollar was currency worth writing home about. A trio of worldly-wise Englishmen, myself included, chose the suspended ceiling as a failsafc hiding place and went off to have dinner – no alcohol included. We returned to collect the stash maybe two hours later and it was gone. A massive search was undertaken in a frozen panic, as the money was in fact proceeds of a gold smuggling operation from Nepal or India, belonging to several Israeli ex-special forces personnel who regularly used the gold-to-currency services between Malaysia and Singapore. As Singapore was a tax-free haven, possessing these amounts was a no-questions-asked matter, although, in India and Nepal, they incurred a five- to ten-year sentence (no parole). Israelis are unable to travel into Malaysia as the two countries have had diplomatic issues, but being British it was a question of flash the royal blue book and over you go – a one-stamp wonder. We were always their troubleshooters if things were seemingly hot, as we could escape with the cash –

quite legally. They trusted us and we held a retainer. One of the English party also had an extended role as an enforcer, but I do not want to get drawn into that here. I was happy being called 'the bagman' and my friend 'the accountant'. The enforcer travelled far and wide, using his Hong Kong residency and colonial status to foster contacts across Asia for the Israelis. But now we had lost a million dollars and the enforcer turned a deathly white. He did not panic but his look told all – we were dead, no excuses.

After three exhaustive hours of searching, we received the expected phone call and the depositor wanted his money back. Ashen-faced, the enforcer told him it was not there for collection.

The Israeli accent at the other end spoke clearly: 'It cannot be like this. Tell me you are joking!'

Within minutes, the gorilla was in the room grilling everyone on the details of the deposit: where was everybody, who went to the toilet during the meal, were any phone calls made or received, who saw us leave, who served us at the restaurant, did we talk to anyone, etc, etc. An Israeli commando stood outside blocking anyone's exit.

It was a desperate situation. The accountant looked at me and I knew what was going through his ex-military mind – should we steam them and get out alive? Luckily, the deathly pale enforcer picked up on the vibe and made a barely perceptible shake of his head. Some time and a gallon of sweat later, we were marched to the foyer to go on to somewhere else.

# A MAID MAN

It was the green mile of the gold-smuggling world, I felt sure. Torture seemed a distinct possibility.

As we passed reception to hand in some keys, the beaming Chinese girl said, 'We think we have a bag of yours. It is locked in the safe.'

She didn't have to ask again as five very relieved men, gushing and charming as you like, helped her retrieve it. It turned out that an air-con engineer was looking at the pipes and removed the tiles, revealing the bag. Only in Singapore. Anywhere else, the UK included, that engineer would have been on his way to the Cayman Islands – one way.

And this was the reason the hard drive, as bulky as it was, was coming with me in a small holdall. Fuck the club doormen and fuck everyone, the hard drive was not leaving my side tonight, or else I would stay indoors. There is no such thing as a secure hotel room. Only when they invent Hotel Houdini with three-foot steel walls and no windows plus a thousand-foot drop, where you are the only key holder, will I believe all the security hype.

The hard drive was glued to my side as my cross-dressing visitors came to collect me.

## From IPTV to TV

From the outside it was just another narrow, red-brick, terraced house typical of Amsterdam. The two black doormen, both Africans, searched us and came to my small bag with the hard drive. A big discussion ensued, as they insisted it was left in the

**117**

cloakroom and I stoutly refused to part with it. The two transvestites argued that it was my work and had to come with me. First we came up with a story that it was my accounts from the ING bank and could not be lost. Of course, the two doormen pointed out the manager had a safe where we could leave it. The discussion went on and on but they were not letting me in, demanding I hand over the package. In the end I told them it contained porn and, if it was lost, I, and they too, would be in some position of danger. They looked at each other, smiled and let us in without another word. People tended not to mess around once the word porn was mentioned, whether it was Holland or London.

Inside the little club the light was subdued, but from the shadows I saw at least 30 men dressed in various female attire, some convincing, others more like the theatrical drag queens of British television. The transvestites, or TVs as they are known, were quite low key at first, chatting in recesses. We ordered some shorts and sat down. A tall woman brought over the drinks on a tray.

My first observation was that this was not going to be like a gay club night. The atmosphere was very different and, as the night wore on, I realised that the TV scene attracted some quite butch men, truck drivers, muscle queens and what seemed to be a large contingent of ex-special forces personnel. It was definitely the sort of place where someone cheeky could find themselves getting a very old-fashioned smack in the mouth. My impression since is the TV scene is probably one of the heavier of the sexual circuits, sort of the Hells Angels of the sex world. I know there are TVs who are not like this, and, although some straight men would expect it to have a gay vibe, that was definitely not the case.

'It's dress code so you'll have to make an effort soon, darling,' said Mars, a transvestite attached to the club, looking at me through false eyelashes.

I was ushered into a changing room where I was derobed by helpers who fitted me into a black dress, stockings, bra and flat heels that hurt my feet. Sitting on a chair, I was given a half-hour beauty makeover with creams, eye-liner and lipstick – the works. I looked in the mirror and saw myself as Dame Edna Everage or Danny La Rue. My wide shoulders looked awkward, and I was not a convincing TV by any stretch of the imagination. Someone stuffed up my bra to give me a bit of breastline.

'Thank heavens it's dark in here,' I said defensively.

'You are not comfortable with it?' asked Mars.

I felt that I just wanted to get it all over with and mumbled something about hairy legs. Perhaps I should have viewed it as a fancy-dress party, but it wasn't. The vibe had an underlying seriousness. We went back to our table, and another round of drinks appeared. I held on to my little handbag containing the computer hard drive. More TVs were spilling into the club. The music was hi-energy or 80s, and I remember the Eurythmics' 'Sweet Dreams' at one stage. So here I was – a transvestite.

Talk of high heels, dress sizes, the best makeup, lashes and nylons became an irritant to my ears. With every comment, it became increasingly tedious for me and I sought the soothing balm of strong liquor, which lessened my uptight inhibitions, helping me to make a bit of an effort. Someone passed around a CD with coke on it. Obviously the club was not overly bothered, as no one seemed to hide the fact. I declined, as one of the party burst out laughing and chided me that he thought I was one of the straightest men he had ever met. Mars chipped in that I was a reverend writing a book on porn.

'Porn-again Christian, eh?' came the cocaine reveller's reply.

Well, there was the title for the book, I thought. Everyone laughed and it seemed the ice had somehow been broken.

'Chop up a few lines; I'm going for a piss.' Mars got up and went off.

I racked them up quickly and for a laugh made one of them into a pentagram, an old Brighton party trick. The TVs were absolutely delighted with this and soon mixtures of ketamine, MDMA and speed followed with the pentagram, the hexagram and other occult symbols whizzing around on mirrors, on CDs and the like. The TVs were very animated, in full party mode.

It took Mars a lot more than just a few minutes to return and when he did he was with his friend Maisie, a stunning brunette of Dutch-Indonesian origin. She was beautiful, with soft skin and all the right curves. Her gender was somewhere between the two, unlike the others around me. Even her movements were seductively feminine. I soon learned that Maisie was a transsexual, having had operations to change gender. She was a very sensitive, interesting person who felt misunderstood for many years, feeling as she did that she had been born into the wrong sex. It was strange to think of a male person feeling totally female, regarding their body as a prison of some kind. I had heard of transsexuals, hermaphrodites and intersex relationships, but had never spared any thought as to why they wanted to radically alter nature to the point where they changed sex. Maisie helped me to understand it but, needless to say, her journey had been extremely traumatic and painful, and her tale was very moving. I suspected there had been a nervous breakdown somewhere. Her eyes were sad and haunting. You have to respect people who decide to adopt their own lifestyle, even in the face of extreme adversity.

Someone burped and the laughter pulled me back to the club again. It was a raucous party and getting messy, and way past my bedtime.

Once changed, I felt like I had been there most of the night but, in fact, had only been in the club for four hours. Tired and covered in makeup, still holding my precious cargo, I caught a cab back to the hotel.

In that time I felt I had learned something about myself, and when people ask me what it's like dressing up as a woman, I always say, 'No stranger than wearing a cassock, my son.' Perhaps I say this to protect myself, or maybe it is a conditioned masculine barrier inside me, but the Dutch trip certainly assaulted my own comfort zones on many different fronts.

Back in London, it seemed I had made my bones; the pornographers knew they could trust me. I had earned the complete admiration of Tony and his associates. But in my mind Maisie's saddened, world-weary eyes stayed with me. And they have done ever since. Maybe in every man there is a woman.

# CHAPTER 6

# GAY SCENE

## Gay Films – The Real Avant Garde

My experiences on the Dutch trip had made me more open-minded and accepting of other people's sexual tastes and mores. I wanted to tackle this project much more sensitively than I had before. Those transsexual eyes bore into my soul.

Already, living in the former bondage dungeon had set me apart. I had dumped my television, no longer saw old friends, never listened to the radio or read newspapers. I was becoming further and further outside society. I could earn a living duplicating DVDs or hustling a photo shoot, and no longer had to interact with the outside world as before. But I knew that, even in this new existence, I could not experience every single sexual scene for myself and so wondered how I would continue to write the book. Part of this story is based on my research into this world, to try to help explain some of the convoluted developments that have led pornography to where it is now. This research acted like a counterbalance to the video business. A sort of marriage between Sol and Luna, to put it into symbolic alchemical terms, that is important to understand because it is within us all. But the gay scene is a very different matter.

Whatever I write about this scene is, of course, an outsider's view of an extremely diverse, complex, vibrant and creative community, and I cannot do it justice. In the day-to-day world, the word gay includes both homosexual men and lesbian women, but in the porn world it refers only to male homosexual content – although it can get confusing because there are sub-genres such as gay-for-pay, i.e. men who are straight but will perform gay sex for money. Their female counterparts are referred to as lesbian or Sapphic.

Sexual acts between members of the same sex have been depicted since time immemorial and can be seen in ancient art and texts. Homosexuality has been roundly condemned in Judaism, Christianity and Islam, but not so in classical Greece, where lesbianism and homosexuality seemed to have gained acceptance as Greek urns and other artistic potteries attest. Generally speaking, in the West, these artistic representations of gay relations were not really viewed as something sinful or pornographic until the Victorian era. However, it must be said that the actual act of gay penetration – sodomy – was condemned in law in most European cultures, due to Christian moral edicts.

During the Victorian era, with the onset of new technology such as photography and film, depictions of any sexual material were deemed corrupting and immoral. Pornography was now illegal. The stern British Empress Victoria and her minions seemed to set the standard for the world, repressing all carnal delights. The harsh treatment of gay men such as Oscar Wilde leaves us in no doubt of the mindset of the period. So it meant that gay porn was very much an underground phenomenon, finding the most inventive methods to disseminate the material. The genre was and still is the most original, groundbreaking and thought provoking of all genres in porn, often being referred to as cutting edge.

The earliest gay film was made in the USA in 1915 – *A Free Ride* – and one of the earliest examples of homosexuality on film was *Le Menage Moderne D'Madame Butterfly*, a French production made in 1920. However, full gay intercourse did not grace the silver screen until 1929 with *The Surprise of a Knight*. These types of movies were the gay equivalent of stag films in the USA.

As time went on, gay pornographers became very clever at circumnavigating the laws of their times. A new era began in the 1940s and 50s, with bodybuilding and oiled musclemen clad only in G-strings. These magazines could be purchased openly from any outlet, so ostensibly the reader could be seen to take an active interest in weightlifting while in reality they were used for other purposes. Bob Mizer was the American pioneer of beefcake, as it was later known, and, by the time of his death in 1992, he had left a huge legacy spanning several decades and over a million images.

By the time the sexual revolution of the 60s had arrived, gay porn was metamorphosing, exploring new sub-genres and creating fresh views of gay life. The advent of cheap 16mm film inspired a generation of new artists to adopt gay themes within their work. Art and porn began to merge in some very experimental pieces, bringing contributions from occultist Kenneth Anger, gay director Paul Morrissey and internationally celebrated artist Andy Warhol. Through this work, many preconceptions about gay men were being broken down and examined. For example, Anger's film showed macho biker initiations between hard-looking, leather-clad men. Beefcake types were now being supplanted by youthful men such as Joe Dallesandro, star of Warhol's *Flesh*, later used on the front cover of the Smiths' first album. Comparing this explosion of creativity and its level of artistry with straight porn, it is very clear that the gay community shows far more imagination and perhaps even ability. To underline this, there is another shining example of shaping forthcoming trends in the film *Boys in the Sand*, made in 1971. It played in a New York cinema, breaking all former adult-movie box-office records, long before anyone had ever heard of *Deep Throat*.

With this new era of sexual liberation, gay publishing had arrived. *Playgirl* was ostensibly aimed at women, but with typical underground ambivalence it could also be seen as the ultimate gay magazine. *Blueboy* magazine began to show more graphic full-frontal nudity. Open homosexuality was here to stay – at least in the West.

Videotape and cheap VCRs hit the market and, like 16mm before them, allowed even more people to join the porn markets. Home movies and amateur footage began to arrive in every genre. On the professional side of filmmaking during this period, gay directors John Travis, William Higgins, Matt Sterling and Eric Peterson were the big names who once again redefined what it was to be gay. Beefcake, moustaches, hairy men were out, and we gradually began to see the appearance of thin, youthful, effeminate types in gay films and videos. At the far end of this trend were youths known as 'twinks'. Across the pond in Britain, mainstream art saw the rise of gay filmmakers such as Derek Jarman, who began to transform preconceived sexual boundaries.

The gay film genre continued to go from strength to strength with the formation of its own awards, associations and recognised directories. The Gay Producers Association, albeit a two-year flash-in-the-pan, made enormous steps forward for those working in the field. The Dave Awards, presented by Dave Kinnick, followed, and were later financed by the Adam Gay Video Directory. If you look at some of the nominees at these awards ceremonies, such as the one for Probe, the filmmakers list is truly worldwide. All of these efforts helped form a cohesive gay filmmaking culture encouraging collaboration and positive support networks, as well as the dual role of promoting stars, studios and their products. GAYVN has its own awards and has been a huge success. Gay filmmakers are perhaps the most avant-garde and they are the leaders in many creative fields, particularly porn. However, recently this surge ahead has been tinged with a darker edge and the gay film world has been dogged by scandals.

### The Gay Film Scandals

Over 60 per cent of gay films released are said to be bareback (the gay term for having unprotected sex). This was generally accepted practice until the devastating advent of AIDS, when bareback became something of a sexual Russian roulette. Studios demanded certificates to ensure participants in the films were free of AIDS and HIV, and some companies decided to ban bareback completely. Condoms were the order of the day at these studios, which effectively made them as safe as possible. Gay filmmakers Steve Brewer and Chi Chi Larue and director Michael Lucas became leading campaigners for a worldwide ban on bareback films. Moscow-born Lucas, who runs New York's largest gay film company, Lucas Entertainment, has gone further in his campaign against bareback films by taking out newspaper ads and enlisting the help of celebrities to appear in cameo roles in his productions. Both singer Boy George and comedian Graham Norton have starred in non-sexual roles in his film *Michael Lucas' Dangerous Liaisons*. Lucas has given lectures at such exclusive establishments as Yale University campus, to explain the philosophy behind his art. All three campaigners have recalled nightmarish scenarios of falsified health papers, arguing their case that only condoms are acceptable for the protection of actors during sex. But the message has been slow to filter down to some actors who continue to have unprotected sex on camera, and they are wholly reliant on the veracity of the health certificates of other actors, which has occasionally led to tragic results.

Bareback has continued to thrive despite numerous campaigns against the practice. It is therefore very sad to hear that horrific stories are still emerging well into the 21st century.

One particularly dispiriting example happened in Britain in 2007, where a gay porn company made a bareback film featuring just four men which has so far infected three young men with HIV. This underlines the fact that, when it goes wrong, bareback is deadly. In the wake of this scandal distributors have withdrawn three of this company's film titles from circulation, making the bareback films even more pointless. But who is to blame in a case like this – the studio, the producer(s) or the actors themselves? Reasoned argument has not won the day, so could the threat of legal ramifications do any better?

Another British bareback producer, Rufus Ffoulkes, caused a furore which landed him in jail for persuading a boy of 16 to have unprotected sex on film. As such, Ffoulkes' film is classified as child porn, because the youth was under 18 (the age at which a person may give consent to be erotically photographed or filmed, under UK law) at the time of filming. Producing child porn in any Western country usually guarantees the producer and or director jail time, but the lack of care shown towards the minor in this case seems highly irresponsible; some might even say it is callous exploitation. Did the young actor fully understand the potential consequences of riding bareback? Hopefully, the fate of Ffoulkes might act as a deterrent to others who seek to manipulate minors in this way.

Elsewhere, the gay film world has had other scandals to contend with, raising further questions on age, the integrity of IDs and so on. The twink genre has come into the spotlight due to the activities of the late Bryan Kocis, who first started his Cobra Productions in 2001 to produce films of barely legal gay material. Good-looking men of 18, 19 and 20 were recruited by Kocis, who founded this strong twink brand with popular stars. Two of the more recognised names were Cobra's Canadian Brent Everette and American Brent Corrigan. The teaming of the two on film was regarded as something of a coup in the twink genre, bringing it to new heights according to some commentators. Young guys 18+ were filmed bringing themselves to climax, and these new quality films yielded Cobra and Kocis much success, shown in volume of sales as Cobra came to be a well-known brand.

But all this success came crashing down when Kocis was later convicted of having underage sex with a 15-year-old boy, which may perhaps explain Kocis's preoccupation with twinks. The affair came to light with a subsequent court appearance in the USA. Kocis's defence was that the boy had lied about his age, but the jury was not convinced and convicted him of paedophilia. Further rumours began to circulate that Kocis had filmed his main stars, Brent Corrigan and Brent Everette, prior to their 18th birthdays. Shortly after, Corrigan publicly stated, via an attorney, that he had acquired false IDs aged 17, so that he could participate in the filming. In short, Corrigan and others were saying that one of the main twink studios was producing paedophile porn, and actively distributing it under the guise of 'barely legal'. The Association of Sites Advocating Child Protection (ASACP) also began to get involved in the snowballing case.

However, before any substantial police investigation could be launched, Kocis was freed from jail and murdered in a particularly vicious attack in Luzerne County, Pennsylvania, on 24 January 2007, when he was stabbed and beaten beyond recognition. Police soon arrested two gay porn actors, Harlow Cuadra and Joseph Kerekes, who were charged with murder later the same year. Cuadra was known to be a twink who rode bareback. During their arraignment, the authorities began to circulate a story that the slaying was part of a gay turf war involving two studios, one of which was Cobra. Prosecutors claimed that Brent Corrigan had made secret agreements with Kocis that affected distribution rights via exclusivity clauses. There were also allegations that certain people had cyber-squatted specific gay twink websites. Police allege that Cuadra and Kerekes hatched a plot to free everyone from all these legal constraints by murdering Kocis. The motive is still a bit uncertain but a whirlwind of rumours swirl about the Kocis case, leaving the twink genre in a somewhat uneasy position in the porn world. Barely legal is one thing, but child porn is universally loathed and despised by all distributors.

## Britain's Stately Homos

Society's attitudes have changed, or have been changed. Riotous queen Quentin Crisp was one man to reject the notion of oppression by subverting verbal abuse for his own devices. (The term 'stately homos' is a quote from a film about him.) But another gentleman I came across during 2005 is even more of a stately homo than Crisp himself; he is a Justice of the Peace (JP) and a true libertine in the most classical of senses. Although he is proud of what he does, we will simply call him JP here to preserve his privacy.

JP was among Britain's first openly gay magistrates, which may not seem such a big deal today but was clearly a milestone in society's development.

I had to find out more and took the liberty of ringing JP for a chat. After a brief introduction, I told him that I was fascinated by his open attitude to all of the different facets in his life, which I found very refreshing.

When I spoke with him, JP lived close to the Houses of Parliament, holding as he did one of the most prestigious filofaxes in town. His wide-ranging contacts included members of the highest circles in royalty, the Church of England, law and politics, and he encompassed gay life wherever he found it.

## GAY SCENE

To be perfectly honest, I still consider JP to be one of the most controversial figures I have ever spoken to, and that is no small boast. He was the most disarming, genial and honest person to talk to, and I respect him for his courage and Promethean nerve.

He has received many honours for a lifetime devoted to Christian worship, charity, human rights activism and championing the gay cause, and he has spoken out on poverty and homelessness. He is also a Freemason and has rubbed shoulders with the English aristocracy. Needless to say, his progress was not always made easy by some, at a time when being gay equated with being in the closet.

Perhaps in light of all of the above, given the restrictions of his background and social standing, it is somewhat surprising that JP decided to run a gay escort agency. He placed himself as one of the main escorts, handing out sexual and fetish services to the rich for money.

As a provider of sexual services, which were meted out to his mainly public-school clientele, it is a wonder that he was not sidelined by the Establishment.

Call JP what you will, but he is no hypocrite. He explained that he saw himself as more of a life coach, a gay mentor to others like himself who wanted to move forward. He said that this was being achieved by his escort service, as barriers could be dissolved very easily, helping individuals to perhaps express things they could not do in public life, in their marriage and so on. Some people who used the escort service simply went to dinner with JP to discuss gay issues affecting them. Other people who contacted him would prefer gay public-school scenarios such as headmaster–pupil-type arrangements. Then there were sexual arrangements – fantasies and role play. JP would always find a way to help move the person forward, he said. He sounded very professional in his attitude towards escorting, or mentoring, as he would prefer to call his services.

What was really mystifying for me personally – and this may reveal more about my views than it does about JP – is why a man of his obvious social standing would effectively be involved in sexual escorting. After a couple of years of mulling this over, the only conclusion I can offer is that JP consciously knew he was breaking social taboos, using his unique social position to do so. In JP, perhaps one is looking at a man with a personal mission – a vanguard of social change – although it may be that he is just pursuing his own sexual gratification, or possibly it is a combination of the two. But his completely open attitude in the face of his difficult social conditioning is what made him so controversial, in my view.

There are literally dozens of gay sites catering for various tastes, but I wanted to check out what was happening in the real world. After locating JP, I felt there must be other scenes going on that were equally interesting for the gay man.

In another part of London, in the yellow terraced houses of the East End, there is a somewhat less publicised escort service. It does what it says on the tin and has none of the frills attached to JP. Here in Mile End is a very discreet, professional escort service that supplies a corporal punishment master, several twinks, a realistic Edwardian study, a prison birching block and a hessian-sacked room for bamboo massage. Housed in a brick-built, Victorian terraced house, CP Services is perhaps the premier service of its kind in the country, maybe even Europe. It is run by Keith, a tall, silver-haired gent with a penchant for running a tight ship, and his services are as specialised as any gay man could wish for. I would describe Keith as friendly, but I could imagine that he could turn his demeanour into severe jailer at any moment. His client list extends to international visitors and he has attracted the top names in gay filming, such as Sam Hogan who uses the CP Services HQ as a film location.

Having been given the full tour by the rather stern master, I was impressed by the realism and authentic atmosphere. My only reservation was the smell of disinfectant that pervaded the house. Disinfectant must be used on all of the implements to ensure that they are completely sanitised for each and every customer. Should the skin break after a hearty birching, then it is vital no infection is passed on, especially as most clients are gay and HIV is at the forefront of everyone's mind.

CP Services produces films called the Boddington series, which are set in a fictional setting of an English public school circa 1950s or before, including cross-country runs featuring twinks in white shorts and plimsolls. There is plenty of dormitory pyjama play between kinky masters and students with its inevitable denouement – the scholastic discipline meted out by uniformed prefects and seriously stern masters, to lads as young as 18 or 19. Since CP Services began, it has attracted a large amount of paid online memberships and thousands in DVD sales.

## Cyber-dykes

No discussion of the gay scene would be complete without some examination of the lesbian genre, more stylishly termed Sapphic. Sappho was the first renowned lesbian in history; she existed in ancient Greece, a resident of the island of Lesbos. (To be a person resident on the island or speaking the local dialect was to be a Lesbian.) She was a poetess, versed in song, and lauded the virtues of womanly love. Her contemporaries called her the Tenth Muse. Arguments have raged over whether her poems were philosophical in nature or purely erotic, but the latter sense seems to have won the day.

Most porn in this genre has been produced by large corporate entities or male enclaves; of course, there is nothing wrong with that, but what if lesbians started producing their own porn for a female audience? That is what Cyberdykes.com has set out to achieve; it is an attempt to cut through the swathe of sites and magazine representations of women's sexuality to reclaim their own genre.

Porn experiments like Cyber-dyke really open up this genre for serious discussion, in both its artistic milieu and the politics of male-dominated lesbian porn, but I soon realised that I could not do the genre justice. In the spirit of Cyber-dyke I thought that a direct interview might be more informative. Very kindly, Roxxie, from San Francisco, one of those involved in Cyber-dyke, agreed to give an interview on the site.

*1) How did Cyber-dyke first come about?*

Cyber-dyke.net started with Zille and her partner at that time, Alexi.

They started their personal fetish site, darkPlay.net. They had a lot of other friends who were interested in getting involved, so they started their own fetish sites and brought them together as the Cyber-dyke network. I met Zille through a friend and soon I had my first Cyber-dyke.net site – FootFemme.com.

*2) Most so-called lesbian porn sites are produced by male webmasters or corporate elements. What is Cyber-dyke doing that these others sites aren't?*

Cyber-dyke is for women, by women and made with queer women's interests in mind. There are a lot of women making porn and a lot of lesbian sites, but we are one of the few that depict what lesbians are really doing in their bedrooms. I do very little directing because I prefer to film women as they actually enjoy pleasuring themselves. This is also one of the few sites with female photographers and videographers. I've never seen another all-female production crew for a porn film.

*3) What do you gain personally from involvement in the online porn industry?*

I personally find that this is the most rewarding job I've ever held.

I'm really happy that I can give a 'voice' to queer women, and show the world what we're really like. I know that a lot of models talk about porn as being a form of personal expression. I find that the adult industry is a great way for me to use my creative skills and work with people, but I don't think of it as some sort of personal artistic expression.

*4) Are there any other outlets in the Sapphic genre that have this edgy women-only appeal, or is Cyber-dyke completely unique?*

I'm aware of two other sites currently, and a few DVDs. Other sites have come and gone, but we were the first and have been online since 2000. Since there are so few women on the business end of the adult industry, and even fewer queer women, I'm not surprised that there are so few real lesbian porn sites and film production companies.

*5) Every porn genre has its own politics and issues. Are there any changes to online porn that this particular site is addressing?*

I'm really not interested in politics and issues. I just do what I do. I make porn that I like. I'm sure that this site is a political statement just because it exists. I don't expect to change anyone or anything. I'm not attempting to make changes. I know that Cyber-dyke is sort of a landmark, but that doesn't seem to mean much in the adult industry. It means even less to the rest of the world.

*6) What do you think about men producing Sapphic material? What do you think when you look at porn made by men?*

Well, I suppose that I have to accept that men are going to be producing lesbian porn, considering that this industry is so very male dominated. I like looking at naked women as much as anyone else, but I get really tired of the mainstream lesbian material. I know that many porn stars are actually lesbians or bisexuals, but you couldn't tell from watching the porn! I'm not entirely sure why mainstream lesbian porn is so appealing to so many. I hope that more people will get tired of the same old typical lesbian porn and come to our real lesbian sites.

*7) Have you been well received by other producers in the adult world? Are you chasing good reviews, adult film awards and those types of accolades?*

We are generally well regarded by other adult webmasters, but there really aren't any awards or accolades for amateur web porn. The AVN awards are for film productions and we aren't doing that. I'm not really interested in accolades anyway. I just want to do what I enjoy.

*8) Among your paying members, I am guessing that men must also join the site. Are men welcome at Cyber-dyke?*

Men are welcome at Cyber-dyke. We have many male subscribers, and many couples that enjoy the site together. I hear from a lot of men that they are also tired of the same old mainstream lesbian porn. I also hear that our sites are the right sort of thing that men can show to their curious wives and girlfriends. I'm really happy when I hear that a woman with a negative view of porn enjoys our sites.

*9) What is your single most defining moment while working within the adult industry?*

Ha! No clue. I think that when I first started in the strip clubs it was a bit of a shock to accept the reality of the adult industry. It may look like what you see in the movies but working here is nothing like that is portrayed. I think my most defining moment will be some time in the near future when I can quit my day job and work in the adult industry full time.

*10) What does the future hold for Cyber-dyke in the years ahead?*

More lesbian porn! I'd like to produce DVDs, but it will be some time before we have the resources for that. And hopefully a girlfriend for me.

**GAY SCENE**

## *Good for Her*

Just so this chapter is not too neatly packaged as gay, I want to throw in an anomaly – a sort of really forward-thinking concept that is not readily pigeonholed.

Canadian sex-shop owner Carlyle Jansen founded a group called Good for Her, a sex shop aimed at giving the highest level of fulfilment for women and the transgender community. Carlyle is actively engaged or perhaps even the driving force behind a very niche movement in porn and lifestyle – blending the two to cater for the fluidity of gender within individuals. Carlyle began this unique journey back in 1995, with workshops on sexual matters. Think sex-toy Tupperware parties combined with sex education and you're almost there. Carlyle expanded to include a health spa, the shop for girls, and of course a decade later she became part of the celebrated Feminist Porn Awards.

The Feminist Porn Awards are not anti-men by any means; singles, couples, triples are all invited to attend, but it is a celebration for this particular niche community. Nowhere else in the world does such a gathering exist. I can only imagine it is a bit like Occulture was, at least to the celebrants involved. A unique platform for people to explore their own scene, in their own way. The film categories for awards sound great too: Boundary Breaker of the Year – *Buck Angel*, Smutty Schoolteacher of the Year (Educational Title) – *Expert Guide to Oral Sex Part 1 Cunnilingus and Part 2 Fellatio*, Hottest Dyke Film – *Crash Pad Series*, Sexiest Straight Film and, of course, not to forget the Golden Beaver Award for Canadian Content, given to Bren Ryder. Transgender entries include: Most Tantalising Trans Film – *The Nasty Love of Papi' and Wil* by Morty Diamond. Toronto must be proud. It seems that in Canada certain artificial barriers are being not only eroded but positively ripped down. The Cannes of the feminist and transgender community has now begun and is in its third year as this book goes to press.

I am saddened and perplexed when I think of all the people who are still sexually repressed, even in our own age of discovery where genetics, computers, nano-technology, etc are breaking down so many boundaries in our understanding of life. My own lines of engagement were strangely scattered in the skirmish, but I needed to know more about sex in order to know more about porn – the circle was beginning to join up. I kept asking why society is so repressed and came up with some unusual theories about repressive culture and the explosion of the libido.

# CHAPTER 7

# THE POLITICS OF SEXTASY

## Our Glorious Leaders Get Horny

Much of our sexual morality is dictated (at least in law) by the government, who decide what is and what is not acceptable. This follows laws laid down in the 19th century and only overhauled slowly with the changes in publishing seen in the late 1950s, along with the repeal of the laws on homosexuality and relaxation of the laws on erotic publishing. In more recent years, much of this enforced morality has been eroded, and it is now much more permissible to be open about sexual preferences and practices. Personally, I feel that the morality of the day should be dictated by the common man and not imposed on us through legislation.

We have inherited through legislation a set of the most

repressive sex laws anywhere in the world, which can result in a conflict between our own sexual desires and what is considered socially and morally acceptable. Often this conflict is manifested in political leaders who find themselves in situations where they are torn between behaving in a way expected of their position in public office and satisfying their own libido. The result is the sex scandal, where both public and private faces are subjected to public scrutiny.

Politicians traditionally have been sold to us as healthy, heterosexual, happily married types. In recent years, the old euphemism 'confirmed bachelor' has been replaced with gay, although there seems to have been little further development. But is that changing?

Furtive sexual assignations have seemed almost inevitable among politicians; as individuals, they are susceptible to the same drives as the rest of us, and are as likely to have sexual liaisons, illicit or otherwise. Sex is a primeval instinct; it may be repressed temporarily if necessary for a variety of reasons, but it will always reappear in the person's life somewhere. If these sexual urges cannot be expressed properly, it may lead to some form of unhappiness, illness or depression. So people inevitably take the chance to satisfy them despite any adverse consequences, and there may even be a thrill factor in doing so.

We are all well acquainted with the political sex scandals that have occurred both here and in the US. In the White House, for example, there was the well-publicised liaison between Monica Lewinsky and President Clinton, and JFK was said to have suffered from the psychosexual disorder satyriasis. As for the British Parliament, MPs have reportedly indulged in plenty of shameful episodes to keep us all rapt, one of the juicier scandals being the notorious Profumo affair which rocked the British Establishment in the early 60s, as well as numerous more recent affairs. Profumo, immortalised in the film *Scandal*, changed the face of British society forever. Before the revelations, it was believed that ministers did not lie to Parliament and men of position did not mix with the louche world of sex parties.

But do not imagine that this is a modern disease. There is nothing new in sex scandals involving government, leading civil servants, politicians, arms dealers, ordinary people and those in between. History demonstrates that the archetypal high-society sex scandal has been and gone, and is yet to be surpassed. Its very name conjures an age, an irreverent frivolity, a satanic aesthetic that Clinton and Lewinsky could not hope to reach in terms of scandal – welcome to the Hell Fire Club.

## The Monks of Medmenham Abbey

The Hell Fire Club was known under various titles including the Monks of Medmenham or Order of Saint Francis. Its founder, Sir Francis Dashwood, a wealthy gentleman in the 18th century, acquired a ruined shell of an abbey at Medmenham, near High Wickham in Hertfordshire. Here sex and the Establishment went hand-in-hand. There has been nothing like it since, or at least no reports of it. These hint at something approaching a modern version of the Hell Fire Club, but it is not quite there yet.

# PORN-AGAIN CHRISTIAN

Dashwood restored his abbey with care, all for the purposes of establishing the right atmospheric conditions for his blasphemous orgiastic gatherings. The abbey itself was decked out in much finery, with an erotic library and furnished cells. Sir Francis, along with his friend Lord Wharton, then set out to recruit like-minded people who wanted to gather at his exclusive Hell Fire Club. Initially, 12 high-society types attended the meetings but before long others joined the throng. Some of the names mentioned among the original members included such powerful figures of their day as Robert Vansittart, Thomas Potter, Francis Duffield, Edward Thompson, Paul Whitehead and John Montagu, Fourth Earl of Sandwich.

It appears Dashwood took the trouble of tailoring each of the celebrants in a monk's habit, or similar ecclesiastical attire. Later the women were decked out as nuns. Whether Dashwood and his Order of Saint Francis was a satirical joke or a seriously satanic movement is hotly disputed to this day. His Holy Book of Prayers used at meetings was composed of 365 different sexual positions instead of sacred verse. Dashwood presided over the debased sexual rites to parody Christian worship, taking on the mantle of Christ. His orgies attracted the highest echelon of the British Establishment, including the soon-to-be Prime Minister Lord Bute. Dashwood himself became Chancellor of the Exchequer, and other participants included the fabulously rich Duke of Queensbury, influential First Sea Lord the Earl of Sandwich, Lord Melcomb, Paymaster-General and son of the Archbishop of Canterbury Thomas Potter, Lady

## THE POLITICS OF SEXTASY

Mary Wortley, Viscountess Fane and Lady Betty Germain, among other aristocratic and high-society types. Among their number were libertines such as Benjamin Franklin and John Wilkes, who was very highly placed among the Order. When the upper-class nuns were scarce on the ground, the resourceful Dashwood hired the notorious prostitute Charlotte Hayes and her entourage out for the orgies. Sir Francis' half-sister, Mary Walcott, was also among the select company.

Every manner of sexual activity was practised, complete with special toys such as the Betsy, a type of wooden rocking horse with one difference – a special dildo carved into its saddle area. Lesbianism was encouraged, as were most other sexual practices. It is said that, when the drunken participants were blindfolded, it was not unknown for incest to have occurred unwittingly during the revels, as some brothers and sisters attended the parties together. It is hardly surprising that such a club should have attracted the likes of the Duke of Queensbury, once described as the most depraved man of the 18th century. It appeared the Earl of Sandwich had demons of his own, seemingly with an unhealthy obsession with raping and deflowering virgins. It was Sandwich who eventually turned against Wilkes for political reasons, and savaged his reputation in the House of Lords. Wilkes was said to have earned the hatred of the Earl after a practical joke backfired. During a Black Mass at the abbey, Wilkes had unleashed an ape dressed as the Devil. For some reason the beast jumped upon the Earl's back, and he was frightened out of his wits in the dark, ruined, candlelit Abbey. Thomas Potter too held a dark secret, as he was supposed to have been a necrophiliac. The list of such perversions went on.

It seems clear that the Monks of Medmenham had cornered a market, perhaps in the same sanitised modern way that the Torture Garden in London has. Perhaps, as more members joined, the Hell Fire Club became more mainstream and it was diluted to a degree. It is difficult to judge the extent of the Hell Fire Club's perversions, but base it on modern people and their desires and you will not go far wrong, in my opinion. I don't suppose everyone there was a dedicated sexual animal or Satanist, and there are even some who argue that Benjamin Franklin only attended in his capacity as a spy. Speculation has always been rife. But the club remains unrivalled inside the world of politics. Perhaps only the Roman orgies may have topped these kinds of antics or high-powered connections.

Scandal did hit the Monks of Medmenham when the Earl of Sandwich made his ferocious attack on Wilkes. Satirists of the time were quick to seize upon the diatribe, demonstrating that the activities of Monks of Medmenham were well-known among their peers. It appears the Hell Fire Club was no great secret in English society at the time.

## Rulers of the East

Conspiracy theorists like to imagine secret cabals controlling the world, but in 19th-century Europe there was a similar

fascination with sex and the harem of the Near East. The
mysterious harem of the Ottoman Empire became a symbol of
Eastern sexuality, but more so in the Western imagination. Not
much was really known about the harem's inner workings until
the early 20th century, but some interesting accounts emerge in
the *History of Sex* by Reay Tannahill.

Slave markets in the Black Sea and Mediterranean provided
suitable girls for the harem, who would then join as seamstress,
musician, coffee maker or accountant and would have little
contact with the Sultan, unless of course they caught his
attention. If they worked their days off as courtesans, eventually
they would be pensioned off or sent to the old harem of the
previous Sultan. However, if they did get noticed by the current
Sultan, then their career paths would change forever. They
would be provided with chambers and treated to a complete
makeover with perfume, baths and nail jobs, and bedecked with
jewels. From here they would be presented to the Sultan in
some secrecy, and could become from there Sultan Valideah
(mother of the next Sultan).

After entering the Sultan's bedsheets by the bottom end and
slowly wriggling upwards to meet him head to head, the harem
girl would use her power as a seductress. Many had been trained
in the arts of love and there were plenty of such manuals
available in the Near East, such as the famous *Kama Sutra* and
an Arabic text called *The Perfumed Garden*.

Although in the West the imagination ran riot with the idea
of the harem as a place of unimaginable, sexually-charged

possibilities, where all tastes could be catered for, in reality it was all about succession to the throne. Wives and concubines intrigued within the rigid system to see their heir go to the top. Draconian laws at certain times meant that the sons of the other mothers or princes in succession to the Sultanate were executed once a new Sultan came to the throne. According to both tribal and Islamic tradition, the first son bore the title kadin, which conferred first rank and heir to the son of that title. The kadin was then modelled for succession to the exalted rank of Sultan. This caused rivalry and scheming within the royal household due to the fact that, once the new Sultan ascended, his brothers and half-brother would be put to death to ensure his safe passage as ruler. It was not the pleasure palace envisaged by countless romantics and poets. Even so, there were some characters who managed to find ways to operate outside of the rigid, stifling system imposed on them, such as the 'Filthy Sultana', so-called due to her interest in sex, whose son apparently had been slaughtered under the rise of the new Sultan. When her husband passed on, she set up a training school for girls who were taught the art of love and rented out to various men. Naturally, when the new Sultan Muhammed IV applied for a girl, he was rejected.

It seems that the Ottoman Turks allowed some sexual freedom, particularly for the wealthy to attain. But, for the Sultan at least, it may have become more of a political baggage than a delight.

## *The Oscar Wilde of Sadomasochism*

Back in modern-day Britain, the combination of politics, sex and scandal rear their ugly heads once again. In 2008, the international media were filled with scandalous revelations about Max Mosley, whose public role as F1 chairman and aristocratic heir collided with the realities of his own sexual desires. When the British press received mobile-phone video of the F1 enthusiast in the midst of his own sexual fantasy, they had their annual field day. But Mosley was no ordinary catch for the press; the tabloids claimed to have caught the son of British fascist leader Sir Oswald Mosley in an alleged Nazi-style orgy.

The *News of the World* ran a story accompanied with video footage on its website showing Max Mosley in a spanking sex orgy with five girls, which is said to have taken place on 28 March 2008 in Chelsea. The paper cited public interest as the reason for the exposé, which claimed Mosley had been stripped naked, checked for head lice, humiliated and treated like a prisoner, before being whipped, shackled and beaten by his tormentors. Two of the girls present also appeared to take a submissive role in proceedings. I don't think any of these details are contested by any party, including Mosley himself, who has stated that he has been interested in sadomasochism for over 40 years, unbeknownst to his wife of 48 years.

But Mosley most certainly did object to the *News of the World* allegations that there had been a Nazi theme to the sexual games, due to the supposedly German nature of the scenario. He also naturally objected to the general invasion of his privacy caused by the covert footage being released worldwide.

It was a sensational story but the *News of the World* claimed it was in the national interest, thereby giving the paper a defence for publishing it in the first place. It stuck to its Nazi theme, alleging that Mosley harboured such fantasies, and would later argue in court that his actions had a 'potential criminal flavour'. The story was dynamite stuff – the son of a fascist being whipped on his bottom in an alleged concentration-camp fantasy. It was a foregone conclusion that papers would sell, and the video downloads were seen by as many as three million people.

Mosley denied any Nazi connotations to the spanking orgy, but it remained a sizzling story. Sex mixed with politics, involving a well-known sporting figure in a sensational tale destined to go around the world. It seemed Mosley was doomed before any defence could be launched, another victim of the fickle public fascination with sex scandals. But he fought back. As a rich and influential man, he elected to defend himself in what could be a costly and dirty fight in the courts. He sought an injunction banning the video, but the High Court would have none of it. At the same time, he appealed on the basis that he was entitled to a private life. He argued that his sex life, albeit a kinky one, was ultimately his own choice.

The newspapers, emboldened by Mosley's failure to obtain an injunction, spread the scandal far and wide. Formula One colleagues began to wonder whether their chairman should continue in his high-profile position in their sport, while Jewish pressure groups condemned his alleged activities as racist, degrading and disrespectful to the memories of those who perished in concentration camps.

A further issue concerned how it was that a supposedly private scenario had been secretly filmed by one of those involved, a lady known as Mistress Abi of Milton Keynes, who, it transpired in a further twist, was the wife of an MI5 officer – an ex-Marine Commando surveillance expert, no less. Whether Mistress Abi had been trained in use of the covert-camera technique by the *News of the World*, as was generally believed, or by her husband is a moot point. But subsequent footage showing Max going into the session is almost perfectly composed, although shot in poorly lit conditions; one has to ask who coached her in the use of undercover video.

Some reports claim Mosley was warned by a former police officer that he was being targeted by a covert surveillance team prior to the scandal breaking, but Mosley evidently continued his spanking activities. Was this a direct warning that the newspaper was out to discredit him, or something more sinister?

Why Max Mosley was exposed remains known only to a few people, and it may simply have been gutter journalism, but Mosley clearly believes he was specifically targeted: 'From information provided to me by an impeccable high-level source close to the UK police and security services, I understand that, over the last two weeks or so, a covert investigation of my private life and background has been undertaken by a group specialising in such things, for reasons and clients as yet unknown.'

The *News of the World* has made money by selling BDSM (bondage/domination/sadomasochism) services in its advertising columns for years and its glib moral stance smacks of hypocrisy. If anyone at all does condone such invasions of sexual privacy, are they in fact waiving their own rights with regard to interference in their own private affairs?

In July 2008, Max Mosley won his high-profile court case against the *News of the World* for invasion of privacy, and the sensational claims of Nazi fantasy were left unsubstantiated. But, crucially, would it have mattered anyway? Sexual fantasy is just that, *fantasy*; it is not meant to be political, rational or representative of our normal persona. In fact, if the facts of porn are anything to go by, it may serve an altogether deeper purpose. The human psyche is rather deeper than the *News of the World* might allow.

Oscar Wilde went on trial in Victorian times for 'gross indecency' and received a two-year jail sentence, as gay sex was illegal at the time. Sadomasochism, even consensual and in complete privacy, is still technically illegal in Britain, so Mosley allegedly allowed an assault on himself. (In Chapter 9, there is a further discussion of this controversial issue, centred on the Operation Spanner case.) Is it possible we could be looking at a 21st-century Oscar Wilde? And will this sound the death knell for invasive tabloid exposés of people's private lives for the purpose of crass titillation? Journalists may decry the muzzling of the free press but the Max Mosley case went far beyond this argument, bringing into question the right to a private sex life.

## Nazi Porn

As was proven in court, the Nazi aspects were completely unfounded in the Max Mosley case, but the publicity highlighted issues surrounding Nazi sex fantasies. Of all the many sexual fantasies, this one seems to remain a real taboo and is perhaps more difficult to understand.

It seems almost natural to suspect Nazi leaders of weird sexual practices. For example, Hitler is supposed to have been a coprophiliac – put crudely, he had a shit fetish. For the record, Hitler was masquerading as a single chap doing his bit for the nation, and was advised not to marry or be seen with a lover. In reality he was seeing Eva Braun, in what seems from the outside to have been a perfectly happy heterosexual relationship. But his political legacy has left us with one of the weirdest conundrums in porn, perhaps also giving us vital clues to our own sexuality.

There are two main types of Nazi porn: the illicit underground films made by high-ranking Germans during the Third Reich, for the titillation of the Nazi elite, although the official Nazi line on porn was that it was degenerate and officially banned; and the post-war fantasies of people (not necessarily Nazis either) featuring the uniforms, Holocaust backdrops and imagery of the Hitlerite state.

Two black and white films still exist, *Desire in the Woods* and *The Trapper*. A woman who appeared in one of the films tied naked to a tree was traced and interviewed, aged 83, in an old people's home some 60 years after her screen debut. She says that she was approached outside a tobacconist's kiosk by a man who drove her to a woodland area, tied her to a tree and filmed her. This man may have been Gestapo. Her interviewer, novelist Thor Kunkel, said, 'She told me she and her sister had had a threesome with a man. I found this a bit surprising.' Kunkel went on to claim that Rommel's crack desert troops traded pornography with the Bey of Tunis, in return for supplies such as water, food and fuel.

So it seems that rogue elements within the Nazi High Command were willing to ignore Hitler, at least in matters of sex. The filmmakers seem to have gone to some lengths to provide this entertainment. Again it shows that censorship, repression and denial do not work for very long, as people were determined to circumnavigate such measures even in Nazi Germany.

Returning to the post-war Nazi fantasies, the story becomes more bizarre as it appears that this genre was most popular not in Germany or a Nordic nation, as one might suspect, but inside Israel. Several Israeli magazines called *Stalags* exist, detailing sexual fantasies of blonde, Aryan women with big breasts dressed in SS uniform, whipping, kicking and humiliating captured pilots of the Second World War. Possibly due to local sentiments, the pilots featured were nearly always American or English in nationality but the women were invariably Nazis from the Third Reich. It seems completely bewildering that such a fantasy could exist in Israel, even to the point where the magazines were openly printed and distributed inside the country. My own thoughts are that, as these magazines were available in the pop culture years of the 1960s and 70s, when nearly half the nation consisted of Holocaust survivors, it may have been an attempt to unleash a national trauma, literally conditioned into the young from birth. I believe it is escapism projected onto a sexual backdrop as a catharsis.

The magazines appeared in a nation surrounded by enemies, fed on a history of surviving the destructiveness of the Nazis, the pogroms, Egyptian slavery and so on. The Israel of the 60s and 70s was very oppressive in some respects, a place of festering conflict, political upheaval and war. When such oppression is passed on in the form of trauma stories, family memories and race memories, it will be transformed into a form of expression that allows life and sexual procreation to continue.

The *Stalags* have been finally consigned to the deep vaults of the Israelis' national library, remaining something of a national embarrassment.

It was time for me to move on. Things had changed for me so much and I wanted to explore the sale of sexual services, especially in the light of the Max Mosley affair. On that day I had the misfortune to read a statement made by the former Archbishop of Canterbury, Lord Carey, who said of the Mosley victory that it 'created a wholly new privacy law' which would allow public figures to engage in 'unspeakable and indecent behaviour' without fear of exposure. He wrote this in none other than the *News of the World*. Of all the many injustices to condemn in Britain, I was astounded that Lord Carey, an influential public figure, chose to sound off about a private, consensual orgy! In my opinion, the former Archbishop would do well to meditate on this.

# CHAPTER 8

# PROSTITUTION – THE FRUIT OF GOOD AND EVIL

## Cock Lane and Other Delights

Prostitution, often called the world's oldest profession, will continue even after the bomb is dropped, because sexual desires are as natural as breathing, and as automatic too. Sex will always trade as a currency; laws and legislation will never stop it, however draconian they may be.

In Britain, the sex industry first saw rudimentary official regulation during the reign of Henry II, who tried to control prostitution in 1161 with some common-sense suggestions. He forbade any brothel-keeper from using force or slavery to keep a girl. As a point of balance, Henry also declared that the girls must not solicit custom – no pulling of horse reins, seizing of gowns, throwing stones, calling out, whistling or trying to attract the attention of potential customers; the king insisted that the girls should only sit passively upon their doorstep to ply their trade. He was obviously aiming for a win–win solution to try to keep everyone happy. Some connoisseurs of the English red-light districts may now understand why the ladies in these areas do not tend to indulge in the more proactive displays seen in Amsterdam, where the girls tout their business by tapping upon the windows, wolf-whistles and frantic waving.

In London, one of the early officially-designated red-light districts, founded in 1240, was the aptly-named Cock Lane in Smithfield. By 1394, any prostitute could have her clothing confiscated by the City Corporation, although, in reality, jewellery was a more preferable asset to seize.

Cock Lane may have raised a smile, but what of Grope Cunt Lane, also in London? (Which at some stage was renamed for the sake of propriety.) Several English and Irish towns and cities have Grope Lanes, Love Lanes and Fondle Lanes where prostitution once flourished. It is clear that prostitution has its own folklore, history, and even its very own political lobby.

Centuries passed with different sovereigns holding completely contradictory views on the subject. The Tudor monarch Henry VII was against the trade and passed edicts to that effect. Charles I tried to suppress brothels too. A deeply puritanical Protestant Parliament, which replaced the Royals after the Civil War, went further still, cracking down on brothels, gambling and anything else they considered ungodly. Pro-prostitution monarchs included Edward VI and the debauched James I.

# PROSTITUTION - THE FRUIT OF GOOD AND EVIL

In more recent times at the height of the British Empire, the country needed to maintain a vast fleet of navy ships in order to protect its far-flung territories. The government provided naval brothels located on specially moored ships, which serviced the sex-starved ratings once they hit the shore. If anyone has ever had the misfortune to be around when a modern naval vessel unleashes its sailors into town, charged as they are on testosterone, they will know that the British Navy were being very canny in taking a little of this male energy away first.

In other countries, the development of prostitution took a different route entirely, sometimes with surprising social consequences. In ancient India, prostitution took on a sacred or spiritual role and was sanctioned by all members of society. Political leaders and spiritual devotees alike saw the women involved as divine vessels necessary in the chain of social and political events around them, not to mention the cosmic consequences of their role too. Huge temple complexes were devoted to such activity.

In the Far East, the role of the hostess, the Japanese geisha, is formal but also challenges some of our rigid social conditioning with its interpretation of the meaning of hospitality, leisure and relaxation, or perhaps in its acceptance of chance sexual encounter in a safe environment. The geisha is a highly skilled, formally trained actress, artist, companion; it is also possible that she is a potential lover – real or imagined.

Today, prostitution is a very sophisticated business with many rungs in its ladder. At the bottom end of the business, lone girls walk the streets to pick up strangers – this is where drug addiction, homelessness and desperation feed the need to sell sex. Elsewhere, more sophistication is employed with the concept of the brothel – a central base from which to operate. Here a modicum of safety can be introduced into the equation, with the provision of maids, brothel-keepers and other staff who can help vet potential clients. Advertising in local newspapers, web personal columns, contact sites and bespoke websites reaches ever more affluent visitors. Specialist areas such as certain fetishes command higher fees and more respect. At the top end of the ladder are the girls who visit offices, hotels, private residences etc and may charge up to £1,000 per client. Supermodel lookalikes only need apply. But this service also demands class, charm, discretion, attention to detail and a first-class service.

## Heidi Fleiss – The Queen of High-Class Hookers

Model lookalikes certainly adorned the books of Heidi Fleiss, a Hollywood madam who supplied gorgeous girls, cocaine and some interesting experiences to rich folk in California. Born on 30 December 1965, she went on to become the foremost madam in Hollywood and the talk of tinsel town. Her prostitution ring served the powerful and famous, making it all the more notorious. In the early 1990s, that all came to an end after she was entrapped by federal agents, who asked for prostitutes and 13g of cocaine for a bogus party. By requesting this substantial amount of cocaine, the FBI ensured that Heidi incurred a heavy narcotics sentence. The US courts found her guilty and she received 37 months, something that her supporters thought very harsh indeed, as essentially she had been set up by federal authorities. Heidi's father Dr Paul Fleiss, a well-known paediatrician, was also sucked into his daughter's arrest, facing charges of laundering her sex-trade profits, although he received a suspended sentence. As for Heidi's rich clients, not one was ever sought for prosecution – further angering critics of her arrest in America, who claimed that the prostitution laws were one-sided to convict the girls, not the boys. Some concluded that the rich in America seemed to be above the law, able to indulge in these supposedly immoral acts with impunity. Supply and demand were debated hotly.

In terms of riches Heidi herself was not far behind, having made a few million dollars in just a couple of years or so. This immense success certainly made her the envy of other madams and pimps, and no doubt even the girls who worked for her. It is just possible that some of these enemies may have helped the feds bring down Hollywood's number one madam by supplying information on her operation, particularly her ability to acquire good-quality drugs.

Heidi was released after a year and nine months, after which celebrated filmmaker Nick Broomfield made a fly-on-the-wall documentary about her, entitled *Heidi Fleiss: Hollywood Madam*. Other films about her exploits include *Call Me: The Rise and Fall of Heidi Fleiss*, and she produced her own DVD on sex tips in 2001 with the late Peter Sellers' daughter. In one deal alone with Paramount, she pocketed a cool US$5 million for her story rights.

In her other business interests, Heidi used her name to open a Hollywood boutique called appropriately 'Hollywood Madam'. This led her to forge ahead with her own fashion street-wear. Fleiss, it seemed, was unstoppable.

Heidi was the talk of the town for some years after her release. Magazines, chat shows and Fox News all made slots for her. Her own stardom in Hollywood, albeit not created by film, was a cause of celebration.

Controversially, she made applications in Nevada to build her own legal brothel, designed as an exact replica of the White House. Legal troubles soon followed when she was once again arrested by police on charges of driving while under the influence of prescription drugs, and plans were put on hold. Instead, Heidi chose the more acceptable business option of opening a laundromat called Dirty Laundry.

It all seems to have ended well enough for Heidi, who has milked her infamous name for all its worth.

In the UK, our nearest equivalent to Heidi Fleiss is probably Elizabeth Holland, who lived in the early 1600s. She was a notorious madam who kept a sumptuous brothel in the City of London, where visitors could feast, take their pick of numerous maidens there or lounge around. Her first venture ended with her incarceration in the infamous Newgate Prison (where the Old Bailey now stands). But, aided by highly-placed clients, she managed to escape before trial and moved to the outskirts of London.

She chose Bankside on the south side of the Thames, out of the jurisdiction of the City of London, as the site of her new brothel, which was constructed inside a ruined manor house. The building had moats, a drawbridge and an outbuilding surrounded by ditches. In circa 1600 Madam Holland bought up the property and set about rebuilding her fortune in prostitution.

Soon the brothel became the talk of London, with luxuriant gardens, pleasant arbours and an excellent hostelry stocked with the best wines and foods. Needless to say her girls were considered some of the prettiest. It is said that she kept a good house famed for its order, hospitality and efficiency, and that her guests included royalty and all of the highest social circles of the time.

It lasted about 30 years, before a change in monarchs led to the storming of this fortress-like brothel by troops. All good things must come to an end.

## Soho in the 60s

Heidi Fleiss may have become the pinnacle of the high-class sexual experience, living as she did in Hollywood, but the geography of prostitution has followed both poverty and affluence. Brothels spring up in both extremities: the first in desperation and the second, more organised type in order to milk rich clients nearer to their workplaces, haunts and social life. Sadly, when prostitution is born out of poverty, it is more likely to bear the hallmark of exploitation, violence, drug addiction, alcoholism, homelessness and crime.

In London, prostitution has moved around to suit the times. Commuters spilling out of Farringdon Station may turn left into Cowcross or Turnmill Street without being aware that this was a most persistent haunt of the London sex trade for some time. Similarly, Southwark, on the other side of the Thames, housed brothels nearly a thousand years ago. Holborn, where the aforementioned Grope Cunt Lane was located, was a name synonymous with prostitution. Looking at post-war London, we can see the trade disrupted then replaced by the new geography of affluence, power, work and the new social boundaries of the late 50s and 1960s. Old trade areas such as Limehouse ceased to be important as prostitution began to go west once more. Holborn too had another flash of infamy for a while, as did Notting Hill and the Strand, but the sex trade settled upon Soho (it had a reputation for being this way for over a century in any case) and that is where British prostitution, pornography and all aspects of the sexual revolution have centred itself ever since. Soho is more than just a red-light district but something of an institution, a tourist trap, a byword in cheap thrills, vice, dirty mags, seedy bars, clip joints, dancing revues and strip clubs.

The name Soho was first derived from the cry of huntsmen who once raced across the fields there after their quarry. Today the word is evocative of the sex industry, but the 21st-century Soho is a pale imitation of its vibrant 60s and 70s incarnation, mostly due to increased police and government legislation to crack down on the various rackets operating there. But, if the government have succeeded in eliminating the dirt, they may also have sanitised the fun – it seems that, in the UK, there is no concept of management or reasonable compromise, as there is in other European capitals. Essentially, the government's moralistically restrictive practices may be part of the problem. As prohibition allows criminality, the authorities may be contributing to a breeding ground for many sins.

The London trade in prostitution was revolutionised in the 1930s by the Maltese Messina brothers – Eugino, Gino, Carmelo, Alfredo, Salvatore and Attilio – who used all manner of tricks to subjugate women into prostitution, gathering them from all over Europe to serve in their regimented brothels. The Messinas are believed to have made untold wealth through their ruthless approach to business: visa and passport problems were apparently overcome by forgery, rival pimps were slashed, difficult customers beaten to a pulp. Their reign of terror and exploitation was ended by a newspaper expose of their activities that effectively led to their fleeing the country and Alfredo serving time. Their empire was aided by Eugino's lover, Martha Watts, who wrote a book about her life called *The Men in My Life*, revealing how she picked up 49 clients on VE Day for the brothers, and was disappointed she did not make it a round 50!

The early growth of adult entertainment, as opposed to prostitution, was centred on the Windmill Theatre, which first opened its doors in the 1930s under the creative auspices of theatre manager Vivian Van Damme. His shows specialised in still posed nude girls who attracted the men in droves. The Windmill posters boasted that the show never closed, not even during the Blitz. Official attempts were made to try to close down the saucy venue, but the wily Van Damme exploited every legal loophole to continue his routine. It only closed voluntarily in 1964, partly due to the more explicit shows surrounding it in the 60s. It seemed the Windmill had had its day.

Its demise had no doubt been hastened when a new attraction opened near to the theatre in 1957. Paul Raymond, a travelling showman running strip nights, opened the now world-famous Revue Bar, where he made the shows somewhat raunchier and carefully took advantage of another legal loophole by creating a private members club, out of the reach of the law. The format was an overnight success and allowed Raymond to build a publishing empire, while acquiring many of the freeholds in seedy, rundown Soho. He soon became known as the 'King of Soho'.

Following Raymond's success, striptease clubs began to spring up all over Soho, although the Revue Bar remained the top venue, with major box-office stars performing in cabaret there. It was always seen as removed from the sleazy side of the sex industry, a legitimate enterprise among a rogues' gallery of somewhat shady ventures, although, in fact, Raymond managed to span both camps, dealing with gangsters but never becoming one himself. He profited enormously from his Soho property portfolio, becoming the biggest property owner there.

## PROSTITUTION – THE FRUIT OF GOOD AND EVIL

By the late 60s, a raft of illegal sex shops had opened their doors for an illicit trade in pornographic magazines. This development was followed closely by the Obscene Publications Squad. Much of Raymond's fortune came from renting his premises to other people engaged in the sleazy side of the sex trade, where prostitution often took place, as well as sex shops. His flagship porn magazines, *Mayfair*, *Men Only*, *Club* and *Razzle*, built up a considerable reputation, making Raymond Britain's leading pornographer.

### The Syndicate

Bernie Silver, a canny Jewish pimp, and his partner in crime – a tough Maltese policeman, 'Big Frank' Mifsud – formed the 'Syndicate', plotting their rise to power from the Coach and Horses pub in Soho. Here they benefited from the 1959 act to outlaw women taking clients in the open, effectively forcing prostitution indoors. After a newspaper exposé caused the sudden collapse of the Messina empire, a void had opened up. Soho was ripe for a new order and post-war money was just about to boom in swinging 60s London

In the preceding years, Silver and Mifsud had faced the prospect of the hangman together but had managed to persuade a jury of their innocence. Mifsud, it seemed, was capable of extreme violence or extreme generosity – most, wisely, chose to appeal to his good side. Together, the pair marched to take over Soho lock, stock and barrel. Their methods were more subtle than the Messinas', but nonetheless profitable. Potential clients would be encouraged to inspect the girls before deciding whether they wanted to have sex with them or not – a far cry from the vicious Messinas, who would threaten, cajole and intimidate clients. The reason for this new approach was that Silver and Mifsud rented the clubs to Maltese hustlers and the rooms above to the girls. Rents of up to £150 a week were not unusual as the pair expanded their empire across Soho. This was a considerable income during the 1960s and it made their fortune.

Before long, the Syndicate became a tight-knit collection of Maltese and some Italian (mainly Sicilian) tenants operating rackets, and funnelling cash back to Silver and Mifsud; Raymond was in the background but was certainly a beneficiary. Another cornerstone of this network was notorious sex-shop owner James Humphreys, whose later revelations would help to indict the corrupt Obscene Publications Squad. At their height in the early 1970s, the Syndicate are believed to have owned dozens of brothels, 24 strip clubs, five blue-movie cinemas and a dozen clip joints, as well as up to 50 sex shops. Behind the empire was a two-pronged approach to keeping on top of things: violence was meted out to girls who did not pay rents, but it seemed their ace card was their ability to foster high-level police corruption.

The Syndicate made millions of pounds every week; it was a huge business believed to have divisional commanders, chief superintendents, even members of the elite Flying Squad vice section on the payroll. This amalgamation of pornographers, sex-shop owners, brothel keepers and enforcers controlled Soho.

## PROSTITUTION – THE FRUIT OF GOOD AND EVIL

One notorious scam perpetrated between corrupt Vice Squad men and the Syndicate was raiding various sex shops to confiscate pornography before later selling back the same stock to Silver and Mifsud. Later, this material would be sold on to men like sex-shop owner Humphreys.

The Soho of the 60s saw the rise of the clip joint, a bar or strip club that presented punters with exorbitant bills for drinks, hostesses, dances, etc. In reality, it was a form of robbery with menaces. Most paid without a fuss, particularly married men and respectable executives who would be too embarrassed to involve the police or a solicitor, lest their family or colleagues found out about their seedy exploits. Such places were set up to exploit tourists and first-time visitors.

Silver oversaw the money side, often using offshore accounts, Swiss banks and Caribbean tax havens to stash their ill-gotten gains. The entire fortune is estimated at around £100 million circa 1972, all of which was made in about a decade or so of concentrated scheming. Convert that into present terms and one quickly sees that they must have been among the richest in London at that time, if not Britain as a whole.

But, as with every criminal enterprise, there has to be a downfall, and by 1972 Silver and Mifsud had run out of luck. Their trial was a sensation, due not only to its salacious detail but also to the unprecedented scale of police corruption it exposed. In fact, one might say that the colossal police involvement was the linchpin to the entire operation. Without the police corruption, Silver and Mifsud may have been arrested long before. Even 30 years later, there are no UK cases in the archives that involve so many policemen falling from grace – perhaps with the exception of the very first Scotland Yard force, derailed by Victorian Masonic corruption almost to a man.

The Syndicate was brought to its knees by the 'Old Grey Fox', Detective Chief Superintendent Bert Wickstead and his team of incorruptible officers, who were appalled by Silver's domination of fellow police officers and vowed to smash his operation.

Silver received a six-year term for living off immoral earnings, and he took at least nine senior policemen down with him. In the wake of this furore, a massive move was made by the authorities to stamp out corruption within the Metropolitan Police force. It led to over 200 resignations, early retirements and unexplained departures due to ill-health. By the time Silver rejoined society, his criminal infrastructure had been dismantled and he was finished as a major force in Soho.

For many years vestiges of the Syndicate remained, including haunts used by Silver and Mifsud like the now defunct Maltese social club on Frith Street, or the nearby Coach and Horses – now just memories of yesteryear.

## Soho Today

It was from the vacuum, created by the absence of Silver and Mifsud, that men such as my contact, Tony, came. To a degree, Soho had remained dominated by the Maltese, although occasionally Sicilian figures would arrive to do business there.

## PROSTITUTION – THE FRUIT OF GOOD AND EVIL

Paul Raymond also held sway over a large percentage of the leases for rent, cleverly avoiding being drawn into bribery and corruption or criminality of any kind.

By the early 1980s, a bylaw had effectively closed many of the illicit sex shops selling pornography. Soon the 70-odd shops there shrank to just 30 by way of an expensive council licensing scheme. While much of the old-style criminality was swept away, at least in theory, it seemed to create a government monopoly on porn. If a film did not have a British Board of Classification listing (again, filmmakers had to pay the government for this licence), then it could not be sold legally within a sex shop. Any shop selling non-licensed products could be closed down by the council or given a strict warning. Closures were not demanded that often, perhaps due to the £30,000 annual licence fee payable to Westminster Council for each shop trading. In a raft of legislation, the government replaced the gangsters but used their lucrative trade to fill Westminster Council's coffers instead. Soho became a bland monopoly, denying the punter the choice he once had. Because of the identical nature of sex-shop products, many once-thriving businesses went by the wayside or had to risk trading illegally once more.

This is why situations arise in Soho which, to the uninformed spectator, seem unfair or unjust. Who can explain why one shop is closed down for selling products that another has in its window only a few feet away? It seems only Westminster Council officials have the answer to that one.

## *Sex Slaves*

Another element who arrived in Soho in the 21st century, partly under the guidance of old guard, are the Albanians. This ethnic group now appears to dominate the business of prostitution with much the same ruthless methods employed by the Messinas in Soho during the 1930s, 40s and 50s. Some of these people came as immigrants, speaking little English, but now have moved up the ranks of their community through mastering the local language and fostering contacts outside of their ethnic group. These brighter sparks are capitalising on their fearsome homegrown reputation for getting jobs done, come what may.

The British police have authorised a report to study the growing menace of the Albanian pimps. Where they differ from other ethnic criminal fraternities is that the men, mostly in their twenties and hailing from northern Albania, are bound by clan ties. They have a strict code of honour called *kamen*, and any member breaking this code is not only shunned but more likely killed. It makes their world almost impenetrable to outsiders, and it makes outsiders easy prey to Albanian pimps who have so far proved to be utterly pitiless in pursuit of money and power. Unless you have some proven track record with these people or can hold them off through fear of reprisal, it seems you are fair game to them. It is dog eat dog, but they do have an internal moral code of their own, bound by years of tradition.

The gangs provide cash to rent properties in Soho, often

owned by the original network from the 60s or their surviving family members. Prostitutes are brought in from Eastern Europe, the Balkans and Russia, and these girls undercut British working girls, apart from the most desperate type of street junkie. As a consequence, Soho prostitution is now reckoned to be at least 80 per cent Eastern European and Russian girls, with the remaining 20 per cent divided between the Balkans and other nationalities, including British nationals. Clients apparently give little thought to how the girls are acquired or treated. Simon Humphreys, Head of the Clubs and Vice Squad in Soho, has said of the Albanians, 'They have a wonderful supply chain.'

Methods used on the women under Albanian control have only recently begun to come to light. Police operations have uncovered a world that is cruel, heartless and brutally shocking. For some girls, often recruited from impoverished countries in Eastern Europe and the war-torn Balkans, their plight begins when they are duped into believing there are great riches to be had in the West. Upon arrival, these vulnerable girls have their passports confiscated, with travel money and agency fees deducted from their first earnings. Some girls have found themselves in a spiral of debt to ruthless gangsters, but even worse tales have emerged too. Girls who travel on false passports are susceptible to being kept in prison-like conditions, forced to work day and night, often being given drugs to keep them going. But some police forces have established that a new, even more evil trade exists – sex slaves, foreign women who have been kidnapped, transported to Britain and held against their will to have sex. Britain, like the rest of Europe, was completely unprepared for the advent of real-life sex slavery.

There were sex-slave stories circulating during the 1920s – tales of white girls held by Chinese opium-den owners for the purposes of prostitution – but it seems these were an urban myth. In the 21st century, the police have been as shocked as the public to find sex slavery really exists.

It is still almost unbelievable that sex slaves could exist in the heart of the UK today. The problem, although thankfully small, has been addressed rapidly by the government with the setting up of special police task forces to combat this new menace. The women forced to work as sex slaves receive no money, no freedom, no promise of a better life and are kept as prisoners, often beaten and raped when they do not obey their criminal slave masters. It appears northern Albanian crime gangs have been central to this evil new business, although I must say none of the Albanians I have encountered are involved in it. The Prostinetta Alliance claim that this was a problem connected with their ethnic group at one time but most of the ringleaders have either been jailed or have fled. They claim that the Lithuanians, Polish and Russians are behind most of it now.

In one case, a 23-year-old Albanian sex slaver was originally sentenced to 10 years in prison but, upon appeal, his sentence was increased to 23 years. The same nationality continued to notch up heavy sentences for sex slaves, violent prostitution and kidnapping. In Manchester, Albert Rama and six co-

conspirators were sentenced to a total of 50 years. In London, major sex-slaver Argon Demarku and fellow gang members saw sentences passed ranging between 10 and 18 years.

## Fallen Daughters of Eve

The Jack the Ripper murders, committed during 1888 in the East End of London, targeted the most deprived individuals, many of whom were homeless alcoholics or living near to starvation. Here in Victorian Whitechapel prostitution took place in the most abject and miserable conditions imaginable and so it was almost inevitable that prostitutes would find themselves vulnerable to the dangers of attack and even murder. But who would have thought that, in 21st-century Britain, we would see an echo of the past in the infamous Ipswich murders?

Over just 10 days, a total of five young women were suffocated and their naked bodies discarded in the countryside. Never before has such a frenzied killing spree been reported in this type of crime. Police as well as the public were stunned by the rapidity of the killings. The police constabulary of Suffolk, a rural area not used to serial killers, were overwhelmed and pressure mounted on them for a result as each new victim was discovered. Sadly, the murdered girls resembled their Victorian predecessors – they were prostitutes of the most desperate, vulnerable type. Every girl found dead was walking the streets, taking any business she could get, largely because they were all addicted either to crack cocaine or heroin.

Because of the prostitution laws in Britain at the time, it meant that girls working together safely from a house could be arrested on the charge of keeping a brothel. This is a serious criminal offence that carries a jail sentence in most cases. While entertaining a client in a house to sell sex is not illegal, having another individual there for safety is classed as brothel-keeping. Inevitably, girls working alone on the streets find themselves being picked up by random strangers in cars. To ensure that the clients are not picked up for kerb crawling, or the girls for the crime of soliciting, this activity often takes place in deserted areas or dark places, thus increasing the danger of attack, robbery, rape and murder. In Ipswich, this law served to aid the murderer Steve Wright. Had his victims been legally entitled to work collectively from a safe house, or brothel, these terrible slayings may have been prevented by simple security measures. Peter Sutcliffe, the man dubbed the Yorkshire Ripper – whilst he targeted a variety of different women, from students to housewives – also exploited the prostitution laws. In the red-light district of Leeds, some of Sutcliffe's victims were persuaded to enter his car for sex. These desperately poor prostitutes were willing to go with Sutcliffe without heeding the caution they might otherwise have observed, if not driven by poverty.

A constant supply of prostitutes walking the streets alone certainly increased the number of victims available to the killer, as well as aiding him by ensuring he could whisk victims away to dark, isolated areas. It was a recipe for easy killing.

In the wake of Wright's conviction, prostitute collectives,

women's groups and more enlightened councillors were calling for a new approach. Various new avenues were proposed, looking at several other European countries and their different approaches to the trade. Germany and Holland legally sanctioned and controlled prostitution in some places, with careful monitoring of sex workers' health to minimise diseases such as HIV. Sweden – where selling sex was not illegal but buying it was – effectively made the client the criminal, not the girl. Finland had taken a tough stance on sex trafficking by sanctioning indigenous prostitutes to set up shop, but making it illegal for foreign nationals to take up the profession. Each of the different approaches had yielded individual results both good and bad, but at least they were attempting to get a grip on the situation. In Britain the legislators continue supporting the Victorian laws, despite the scandalous results that allowed both the Yorkshire Ripper and the Ipswich maniac to kill with ease.

But it seems to me that more members of the general public than ever before have begun to realise that management of an issue is better than living in complete denial. A tide of change has begun with the first step, the questioning of the moral dictatorship that governs the sex laws. An open debate on the nature of prostitution, discussing some of the underlying factors that drive the trade – such as drug addiction and sex slavery, as well as making safety paramount in all cases – has begun in earnest. Women's groups and anti-trafficking initiatives have begun to take their views to Interpol and government bodies across Europe. The moralists continually state that it should remain illegal, but seem to offer no suggestions as to how those poor girls in Ipswich might have protected themselves – short of not working as prostitutes, which will never be an option while drug addiction and poverty force them into doing so.

One particularly misguided strain of moral opinion within the British government suggests that prostitution should be completely outlawed, with any girl found working in the business given a rehabilitation order along with a possible automatic three days in jail. This, of course, fails to acknowledge the underlying factors that drive women who work the streets, such as hard drug addiction and cash problems. If the government forces the trade further into the shadows, it will only increase the dangers for those women.

Lessons can be learned from Ipswich. The most salient one is that the laws on women working together in safe houses need to be relaxed. If this is the one single change, I believe it will be a milestone in protecting the lives of the estimated 80,000 sex workers who work in Britain every single day.

## CHAPTER 9

# THE LAW – NON-CONSENSUAL PUNISHMENT

### *Reading You Your Rights*

I sincerely believe that the sex trade, like any other business, must have regulation to protect both consumer and purveyor. Tax money would be the government's reward for overseeing the trade. The general public would gain too, as there would undoubtedly be less crime associated with it and a positive boost to health issues.

There are those who regularly fall foul of the current legal situation regarding the sex trade. Some I have great sympathy with, particularly prostitutes working within the UK. But there are several cases that present difficulties as they are not black and white legal issues, requiring more than punitive measures. Some may be repulsive and disgusting, but that should not make them less valid for all that. I do not claim to have all the answers to the difficulties in regulating the sex trade, but I am throwing these cases into the mix to stimulate thought and debate.

### The Scat Man (Muckraker)

Coprophilia, or scat, is a very unusual fetish, involving people who defecate on one another, or perhaps squat over glass-topped coffee tables as the person below gets off on the scene above. How this fetish came about I have no idea, perhaps psychologists will unlock the secrets of this paraphilia in years to come. I suspect it is born out of childhood fantasies, like most of our lascivious desires, but to me coprophilia seems one of the most challenging. I must confess that, even while writing this book, I did not actively search out contacts in this field. Understandably, it is a highly specialised niche, with few prostitutes offering this service, and it seems that those who do may command their own price.

On the net coprophilia is big business. Frenchman Stephane Laurence Perrin, who lived and worked in Sussex, bought an existing coprophilia website and hosted it in the USA. It is alleged that a London police officer, while surfing the web, chanced upon the site. After seeking guidance from Crown Prosecution Service lawyers, he found that the police could actually make an arrest on the basis of an obscure loophole in the law. The money from Perrin's American online billing system was wired back to the UK. By banking the money on these shores he was breaking UK obscenity laws, and he was therefore arrested. Perrin could hardly believe it.

Although none of the material was filmed here, stored here or broadcast here, because it could be viewed here and because Perrin was a resident banking here, he could be arrested and charged. (The Frenchman may have been justified in thinking, 'Merde!')

However, the trial did not go as planned and many of the obscenity charges were thrown out, as the offending material was scheduled to be sold through a password-protected site that demanded payment to access the secure areas. This saved him from a very long jail term, although he still received a staggering two and a half years' imprisonment for the only conviction that could be secured against him, which was for the free tour open to all surfers.

Home Office minister Vernon Coaker took a very active interest in the case, later proposing drafts of further papers to restrict what people may or may not view on the internet.

Perrin had been unable to maintain a legal defence, but one very useful fact emerged. The obscenity laws exist to stop filth spreading, i.e. they are there to prevent others being depraved and corrupted by pornography. It was noted by the trial judge that the only person who had complained about the material was the London PC. At the same time, he presumably didn't consider himself to have been depraved or corrupted as a result.

Nonetheless, the jury convicted Perrin on the basis that someone *may* have seen the material and may have become hypothetically corrupted as a result. To me, it is clearly another grey catch-all offence.

In reality, Perrin's prosecution seems something of a technicality in law, so I am sympathetic towards him as he could argue that he took reasonable steps not to break the law within the UK.

Perhaps, if nothing else, this ought to be a cautionary tale to anyone who would dare enter the glass-coffee-tabled world of the coprophiliacs.

## *Operation Spanner*

In an entirely different scenario, the legal implications were even more serious. It all began in the 1980s, when a group of homosexual men met to engage in sexual activities such as bondage, domination, sadism and masochism. These informal get-togethers involved severe whippings, punches, lacerations and genital torture. It is unlikely that any of this consensual activity would have come to light were it not for one of the participants filming it on video. The video then fell into the hands of the police, who seized it, thought they were viewing a murder and sprang into action by interviewing dozens of gay men. Neither the police nor the men involved could ever have thought that the case would be the subject of debate for years to come. The police operation launched to investigate the supposed murder was called Operation Spanner, encompassing an investigation, prosecution and convictions, and a series of appeals, that have divided the sex trade, gays, courts, police, civil rights workers, European human rights judges and internet pundits ever since.

Most of the officers and interviewees believed they were involved in a serious murder investigation. In effect, the police thought they had possession of a sort of BDSM snuff film. That at least is the official version of events. Detractors claim that the expense of the investigation led them to try to achieve results come what may, even when they realised that no murder had taken place.

Much time and energy was put into the police investigation, although it soon became clear that the video showed consensual BDSM sex games between gay men conducted in complete privacy. None of those involved in the painful episode had complained to the authorities or had cause to complain; there were no serious injuries or medical treatments as a result, and no psychological implications either.

However, following a series of raids and a number of arrests, 16 men were charged with an array of offences, and a further 26 were cautioned. The charges included actual and grievous bodily harm, and one man was charged with running a disorderly house. In retrospect, it seems that prosecutors wanted to draw a line in the sand on what is acceptable as sexual play and what is considered torture. To this end, they drew upon Victorian legislation regarding bodily harm to effect these prosecutions.

Critics of Operation Spanner point out that a lot of public money had been spent garnering this evidence; it is estimated to have cost up to £4 million, a very large sum even by today's standards. Operation Spanner went to court with the serious intent of jailing all the men involved for their sexual activities as, in the eyes of the law, such harmful activity was morally wrong as well as sadistic. The more cynical observers claimed Spanner was nothing more than saving face for the police, who had made a gross error of judgement in launching a murder inquiry. Many people were now involved in this most sensational of court cases. To some it seemed as if Spanner had opened up the bedroom door to the state. Police and politicians, some argued, could now dictate what happened in the sex lives of consenting adults.

The trial was heard at the Old Bailey, London. The defendants included the well-known Mr Sebastian, a proponent of body mortification and tattooing, Colin Lasky, Roland Jaggard and Anthony Brown.

In 1989, Judge Rant decided that a plea of not guilty through consent to actual bodily harm was not a legal defence, and the men pleaded guilty with mitigating circumstances on advice from their solicitors. Sentences ranged up to a maximum of four and a half years.

In 1992, Lord Lane of the Court of Appeal heard their cases. Again, his ruling concurred with Judge Rant, and the men lost their appeals. In the December of that year, the House of Lords heard a further appeal where there was something of a split decision on whether the case was about violence or sexuality.

The case eventually went to the Court of Human Rights in Strasbourg for a verbal decision. But already the strain for some of the appellants was too great. Colin Lasky, having endured imprisonment and the associated prolonged stress, finally died of a cardiac arrest.

As the case dragged on, some of those involved began to see it almost as a mission to fight for universal personal freedom. The police, meanwhile, were staging well-publicised raids on spanking magazines and private SM parties, possibly to form some sort of cohesive background to what they were fighting against. However, most of these raids resulted in the cases being thrown out of court.

The decisive victory for the men, now released from their jail terms, was the final judgment by the Law Commission stating that, short of causing permanent physical injury, SM activity should be legal provided it is consensual. Back to square one again. Nothing had really been resolved for either the authorities or the people involved in SM.

So heated was the furore that a special trust called Spanner Trust was set up by gay groups, supported by solicitors and barristers concerned by the state interference in consensual sex between adults. Other well-known sex campaigners, such as Tuppy Owens, put their names forward as patrons of the Trust.

Spanner – both Operation and the Trust – have certainly opened up a debate. When I attended a corporal punishment shoot, I too was shocked until I realised that the girls in it really got off on pain. In fact, they thrived on it. There is a question of liberty here. I like the idea of complete freedom, but I am still wary of branding and severe bodily mutilation. Should there be laws governing extreme BDSM or are people entitled to decide themselves what they wish to subject their bodies to? It is a very fine line, but I think the last word ought to go to one of the defendants, former scientist Roland Jaggard, sentenced to three years under Operation Spanner: 'The most important thing in my life during these times was my complete lack of guilt about any of the SM play in which I had engaged. Because of this I was determined not to kill myself no matter what happened to me. I knew I was not a criminal, whatever the judge and the law said. So sure were the police and the judge that "The full consent of everybody concerned" was no defence to the charges of assault that it took two weeks of legal argument to reach the "Consent is no defence" judgment by the aptly named Judge Rant! As a result of Rant's judgment (following the advice of our legal teams) we all pleaded guilty to our charges. On 19 December 1989 I was sentenced to three years in prison for consensual SM sexual play. I broke down in tears after I was taken to the cells.'

## The Longhurst Campaign

One particular case seems to echo the above concerns about freedom to engage in consensual sexual practices, and has its origins in a murder committed in Brighton. In its wake came the Longhurst campaign that sought to change the face of what people may view on the internet, and seemed to infer that the state was right to regulate certain erotic desires. It is an extremely controversial campaign, leading many involved in alternative sexual culture to conclude that Britain is becoming a police state. Contrary to this view the tabloids lauded the campaign as right and just.

Musician Graham Coutts dated local music teacher Jane Longhurst, after contacting her online. Like many people they met after exchanging emails. However, in this case, at the end of the date Coutts strangled the pretty teacher, stashed her body in a storage facility and then transported it to Pulborough, West Sussex. Here, in deep woodland, Coutts tried to burn the corpse, then buried it in a shallow grave in an attempt to avoid detection. Jane's body was later found by a dog walker, who alerted the police to the grim discovery. Detectives soon matched the body to the disappearance of the missing teacher.

It was not a difficult murder to solve. Jane's computer quickly revealed she had arranged to meet Coutts, and from there the police had the prime suspect. Coutts admitted they had been on a date, but his own computer viewing history yielded much more damning evidence; it was clear he was a lover of necrophilia, strangulation and extreme porn sites. Strangulation was the method of murder, so it seemed the police had not only found the killer but had the motive too. They believed that Coutts had become fixated by such extreme pornographic imagery and had strangled Jane, acting out fantasies he had cultivated online.

Coutts maintained that he had indeed dated Jane, and that she, like him, had enjoyed being strangled during love play. He was adamant that her death was a terrible accident. Despite his defence, the prosecution revealed to jurors that Coutts had visited the body several times, captured on CCTV near the entrance to the storage facility. Again because of his frequent interest in necrophiliac websites, it was inferred that he continued his relationship with the corpse. Finally, when the decomposition of the body was so advanced, he was forced to dump the mortal remains. He was clearly a murderer with a necrophiliac obsession. The jury found Coutts guilty and the judge passed the mandatory life sentence. Coutts' appeal against conviction has subsequently failed.

To what degree Coutts was influenced by the internet is unknown. Perhaps, like many killers, he had harboured these unhealthy obsessions for years before acting on them. For other people, it is possible that going on such websites may vent their desires and help them to avoid killing people; or perhaps not. Of course, no one can say for sure.

Naturally, Jane's devastated mother, Liz Longhurst, had been appalled at the perverted notions of necrophilia. Not only had her daughter been cruelly murdered but, compounding the family's suffering and distress, the corpse had been defiled. The family were led to believe that the cause of the murder lay firmly rooted in the internet, as were the jury and the public. Police and prosecutors painted a picture of a man addicted to necrophiliac sites. They claimed that internet porn was to blame for the murder, as it had triggered Coutts to kill.

After Coutts received a life term for the murder, Liz Longhurst began a campaign for a change in the law, petitioning Parliament for a complete ban on extreme pornographic websites and downloading their images onto computers. She was supported closely by Reading West Labour MP Martin Salter. The Longhurst campaign focused chiefly on strangulation and necrophiliac sites, but also included other unnamed genres classed simply as extreme or violent. However, what is extreme to one person may not be to another, and echoes of the Spanner case reverberated once more, striking fear into the hearts of webmasters and mistresses, magazine editors, fetish clubs, models and homosexuals – not to mention the thousands of private individuals who used these sites, all of whom feared an internet Inquisition that could make them the next targets in a moral crusade.

The Longhurst campaign led to a consultative White Paper, a proposal to change the law to encompass possession rather than production of pornographic material. An individual downloading a few images of something like necrophilia or strangulation could now be prosecuted, even if the site was produced abroad. But because of the grey area of violence to women, also drafted into the White Paper, other fetish websites felt they had reason to fear that they too would be criminalised. Does binding people with rope, spanking, verbally abusing, gagging, dripping candle wax on to naked bodies, etc, constitute sexual violence? They may be kinky, but should these activities be classified as dangerous too? Are they illegal *now*? Should the government be allowed to dictate what consenting individuals do in their sex lives?

The effects of the Longhurst campaign led to the formation of

Backlash, a BDSM-inspired group who wished to clarify legislative semantics and avoid a catch-all law.

Liz Longhurst and Martin Salter won the day and saw legislation passed to ban necrophiliac and strangulation imagery from being downloaded onto any computer within the UK. To the dismay of Backlash, there was still a grey area concerning possession of violent and extreme pornographic material allowed to go through as addenda to the Act of Parliament. Once again, it seemed repressive, neo-Victorian Britain had triumphed over liberty.

My own thoughts are clear on this matter. Firstly, Coutts should be jailed for life as he is plainly a murderer and deserves no quarter whatsoever. It is paramount that the authorities should attempt to understand why he killed Jane Longhurst. Did the internet play as big a part in the murder as the authorities insist? But secondly, I believe evidence gathered in more liberal countries contradicts the Longhurst campaign's rather simple view on pornography. This alternative research suggests that acceptance of pornography plays a big part in actually reducing sex crimes such as rape.

As a somewhat dark footnote, when I made my first documentary I met a 23-year-old woman from Brighton who enjoyed being strangled in sex play. She told me she worked as a prostitute to supplement her meagre student allowances, and many clients strangled her for pleasure, both hers and theirs. However, she felt compelled to give up sexual strangulation after a near miss, although she longed for it as much as for normal intercourse. She also observed that, had it all gone wrong, she would no doubt have been described as a murder victim and her lover may have been jailed for life. This young woman may have been a regular visitor to strangulation websites and maybe she still is.

I do not suggest for one minute that Jane Longhurst enjoyed erotic strangulation, but the Longhurst campaign seems to deny the possibility that others might do.

However, when its own devotees acknowledge its dangers, perhaps this controversial fetish is just too dangerous to allow.

## The Very Questionable Case of Janie Jones

The trouble with passing ever more stringent laws on the sex trade is that we may often assume, in my opinion erroneously, that those enforcing the policies are untainted by those passions that arouse the rest of us. The case of Janie Jones seems to expose a very dangerous precedent in law and may be a warning to us all.

Janie was a London madam who ran a stable of successful brothels in the 1960s. Extrovert to the point of exhibitionism, she attended galas with her breasts exposed and drove a pink Rolls around to the many sex parties she organised. Painted in some circles as a rather fun-loving, somewhat mischievous soul who was very misunderstood, to the dryer British Establishment Janie was seen as a brothel-keeper and a blackmailer.

Her first serious brush with the law came in 1966, when she

was charged with blackmailing a man known only as Mr A. He alleged that Jones had threatened to inform his wife of his infidelities with vice girls she employed. Prosecutors claimed that a demand was made for £1200, no small amount in 1966. Tales of Mr A's sadism and hiring several girls to swim in pools like fish may have titillated the public, but it seems there was no legal case to answer. Jones was never convicted, but she had made enemies.

One month later, she was once again arrested. This time she was simply charged with running a brothel. During her trial it transpired that the police had fabricated statements, and Janie was once more acquitted.

It is possible that her high profile in London did not help to endear her to the authorities, who may have thought that she was provoking them or contemptuous of the law. There again, the police may have been genuinely concerned that a person given to blackmail should be allowed to continue in such a line of business. Clients of brothels may be easy victims in blackmail plots and public exposés, as we have seen in the Mosley affair.

In 1972, the *News of the World* tabloid ran a sensationalised story exposing a sex scandal at the BBC, involving Jones and her girls. Trouble reared its head once more. This time the newspaper claimed that Jones was hoodwinking the girls, effectively tricking them into having sex with DJs and other staff in the belief that they would get jobs on the radio and in TV. Although the good name of the BBC had been temporarily besmirched, it seems the untouchable Jones had once again slipped away unscathed.

But the final showdown came two years later, with a trial at the Old Bailey. Janie Jones was charged with several offences including blackmailing a peer of the realm, referred to throughout the trial as Lord Y. The court heard that the rather kinky Lord Y enjoyed girls dressing up in school uniforms and carrying teddybears. Jones was found not guilty of blackmail, but she had finally been convicted of controlling prostitutes.

Before passing sentence, the presiding judge, Alan King-Hamilton, commented that Jones was the most evil woman he had ever encountered. At that time, such an offence might have been expected to carry a sentence of somewhere in the region of a year's imprisonment. To the amazement of the entire court, Judge King-Hamilton handed down a draconian seven-year sentence. The sentencing was bizarre and bewildering at the same time. Jones herself was stunned by the severity of her term. She was not alone in that view.

## Epilogue: *The Judgement Is the Mirror*

Evidently, the interpretation and enforcement of our sex laws are riddled with uncertainty and raise questions about the very notion of freedom and liberty. In my opinion, they have the potential to foster corruption and the arbitrary enforcement of often outdated ideas of sexual morality. While the laws undoubtedly attempt to suppress the most extreme sexual elements, as demonstrated so clearly in the Spanner case, they can create a minefield of issues surrounding personal liberty and choice. Whether one approves of the activities of the Spanner men or not, there are certainly some grounds for suggesting that the police may have been overzealous, if not arbitrary, in their prosecutions, as critics have claimed. And, in my opinion, the seemingly kneejerk legislation introduced as a result of the Longhurst campaign has further muddied the waters by creating ever more complex grey areas for internet content providers and users.

I believe it is time for a completely modern overhaul of the sex laws, overseen by a panel of open-minded, well-informed people drawn from all walks of life, including those working in the sex industry at all levels. Lord Longford, although a critic of pornography, chaired such an initiative in the early 70s. His report was far-reaching and involved a wide cross-section of society to debate the issues. The dialogue may have remained just that, but it was at least a proactive move in the right direction. Without such a cross-collaboration of people, the British sex laws can never truly be just.

All other institutions in British society have transformed to meet the modern age: schools, colleges, prisons, hospitals, social welfare, military, even the police force. I believe we should demand the same modern approach to the sex industry, which would create an enlightened, up-to-date sex trade on a par with some of our very civilised European neighbours. A humane sex trade that protects people, eradicates disease and prevents exploitation. It is now time for Britain to truly join the 21st century.

# CHAPTER 10

# PORN AND
# THE MOB

## *It's a Hit*

The US Mafia moved into the newly money-spinning porn
market during the 1960s, which provided a lucrative alternative
to the narcotics trade. Mafia intervention began mainly through
investing in and controlling peepshows, porn cinemas and the
strip-club industry. Later came film distribution, when rival
theatres and chains all had to buy their product from Mob
sources. By the 1970s, the acknowledged kingpin in this field
for the entire East and West Coast Mob was a man named
Michael (Mickey) Zaffarano, a captain in one of the five major
Mafia families whose father had worked under Al Capone.

According to police reports, Zaffarano was a member of the
Bonnano crime family, but also worked closely with the

Gambino family of New York. His own business interests included a chain of cinemas called Pussycats, where men could hire private booths. If you made porn in California, at some stage it filtered through the Zaffarano network.

His style was one of arbitration, at least within the Mafia world, as he seemingly had the skill of overcoming internal Mob politics and disputes. He always attempted to encourage cooperation among different factions for the mutual benefit of all parties. Zaffarano made a lot of money for the Mafia, but by all accounts he was not a man to cross.

Men like Zaffarano had set up a sophisticated multi-million-dollar industry across the States. Everyone was happy taking a piece of the pie. Other Mob captains like Robert 'Dibe' DiBernardo, a made man in the Del Cavalcante family (on which the *Sopranos* TV series is believed to be partly based), and Ettore Zappi of the Gambino family also had stakes in the industry. In New York, the Genovese crime family – sometimes referred to as the Ivy League of the Mafia, due to its prominence and power – saw the underboss who would become acting leader, Matty 'the Horse' Iannellio, controlling most of the sex shops and gay bars in New York. These differing factions were all collaborating to control huge swathes of the American porn industry.

Everyone got on, largely due to the peacemaker Zaffarano, who was greatly respected through his time-served apprentice in various Mob rackets.

Another Mafia faction were the Perainos, who were actually a branch of the Columbo crime family of New York and made their mark during the early 70s producing the classic *Deep Throat*, starring Linda Lovelace. To this day, *Deep Throat* is probably the most famous sex film of all time, making it a household name across the globe. The film made Linda Lovelace one of the most celebrated porn stars for decades to come – and included the most famous acts of fellatio.

*Deep Throat* opened for business in 1972, appearing in 300 cinemas simultaneously. It was an instant sell-out, pushing normal Hollywood films into the shade; both *Cabaret* and *Shaft* were outsold by the porn flick at the box office. Net profits on this film, made on a backstreet budget of US$24,000, were now reaping major Hollywood millions. The film made the Perainos very wealthy. It was also a watershed because it is the film that created porn chic. (Think *Boogie Nights*.) The Perainos were quick to keep everyone at bay. Director Gerard Damiano had a share in the film but was bought out quickly; wisely, he sold out cheaply without any fuss. Notorious porn pirates like Bobby De Salvo were stopped in their tracks, only to find themselves working to promote the film in the theatres. Everything was changing. The FBI got involved when it became clear that organised crime was controlling the industry and an era of raids, prosecutions and a raft of new laws began. From 1975 onwards, the authorities began specifically to target porn, as they felt that organised crime profited from it either directly or indirectly.

The Perainos went on to have legitimate ambitions in the film world, handling distribution for *Enter the Dragon* starring

Bruce Lee, as well as the gore classic *Texas Chainsaw Massacre*. As word went round Tinsel Town that they were mobsters, however, the major studios tended to keep them at arm's length.

*Deep Throat*'s actors and producers were soon indicted and brought to trial. Several Peraino family members received short jail terms or fines for interstate porn distribution. At least one police informant was murdered during this lengthy police investigation. Years later, porn pirate De Salvo disappeared, never to be seen alive again, and it was rumoured he had wanted a bigger cut from *Deep Throat*'s profits.

On the other side of the coin, one of the actors, Harry Reems, appeared to benefit from his porn-chic image, as his defence fees were paid for by Hollywood actors Jack Nicholson and Warren Beatty.

But the prosecutions continued as other leading actors, such as John Holmes, were leaned on by police, desperate to make headway in their investigation of organised crime's role in porn. Holmes was the biggest actor of the 70s and 80s, apparently in terms of both box-office success and penis size. He became heavily addicted to cocaine and was offered a stark choice – three years in jail for pandering (the US term for inciting girls into prostitution) or working as a police porn informant. He chose the latter. It may sound like fair game, but the charges of pandering were increasingly being used as a lever on model agents, casting managers, producers or anyone else who hired actors to star in porn films. It seems Holmes was a nice guy whose life spiralled out of control through drugs and destitution. During his time as an informant, he helped bust many porn studios not connected with organised crime and was also alleged to have given a lot of information on the Chicago Mob. Holmes also miraculously survived a sordid porn-cum-drugs affair known as the Wonderland murders.

Unlikely peacemaker Zaffarano met his untimely demise during a police raid in his New York offices on St Valentine's Day, 1979. Police found him running away with an armful of porn tapes. In the excitement he died of a heart attack. Zaffarano's sudden death created a void that opened up the old inter-Mob rivalry, and the American porn industry began to change. In the words of porn expert Luke Ford, 'Zaffarano's death created a power vacuum in organised crime's now international porn operations, touching off manoeuvring among the main Mafia families for dominance of the sex trade.'

The first major Mafia assassinations that followed the death of Zaffarano were *Deep Throat*'s own Perainos. Assassins chased them down the streets of New York. Joey 'the Whale' Peraino survived but his son was killed by a shotgun blast. A nearby householder had her head blown off in the attack. Six weeks later, one of the alleged assassins, Henry Pastori, was killed.

*Deep Throat*'s distributor, Junior Toricho, was run over in Vegas; his body was shoeless. A somewhat dubious official report stated it was a traffic accident. Few believed it; the porn-world rumour was that he was being chased to a spot where a car could slam into him. There were few who mourned the passing of this Mafia bagman.

When John Gotti took the reins of the Gambino family in the 1980s, an ambitious underboss began telling tales on Robert DiBernardo. In short, he related that 'Dibe' was spreading bad rumours about Gotti behind his back. Mafia hitman Sammy 'The Bull' Gravano picks up the tale in *The Other Hollywood*: 'Dibe came in. He said hello. He sat down. The old man Paruta got up, and I told him to get Dibe a cup of coffee. He got up. In the cabinet there was .38 with a silencer. He took the gun out … and shot him twice in the back of the head.'

Later, Gravano and another man disposed of the body. No one knows why he was killed, but some have suggested it was his power within the porn world that made him too big for Gotti. If he rolled over for the witness protection programme it could have spelled the end for a lot of top people. The underboss took over a lot of Dibe's porn organisation.

Some of these hits were sensational headline grabbers. Pornographer Teddy Snyder was gunned down in front of his Rolls-Royce holding a tiny vial of cocaine. As soon as the word porn came into the death, the public understood that the Mafia were behind it. Snyder was the acknowledged Godfather of the US peepshow business, although it appears he had been trying to leave as profits were down.

Elsewhere in Chicago, in 1985, peepshow owner and Mafia porn film distributor Patsy Ricciardi was found murdered in the boot of a car. Ricciardi had been inspired to convert most of the rundown cinemas in the mid-West to adult usage.

Much later, in Chicago, the FBI charged one of the nation's

largest distributors with shipping obscene materials across state lines – a serious federal offence. Reuben Sturman was acquitted and remained a major player. Years later, he got another not guilty for bombing rival stores, but was found guilty of conspiracy to extort money from adult book stores through fear and violence. He escaped from his cell but was recaptured in Disneyland with a suitcase full of dollars and a loaded gun. He died in jail. As his life was unravelled, it was found he had had close contact with Dibe.

The old guard was all but gone by the beginning of the 90s, with the exception of the Genovese family, and a new era came to pass.

## Mafia Scheming

'We need guys like Martino and LoCascio who can do more than killing' – this quote, which is taken from an FBI wire tap listening into the conversation of Gambino Godfather John Gotti, refers to the biggest consumer con in American history. It reveals just one organised porn conspiracy and gives an insight into the vast profits that are made in such criminal ventures.

Richard Martino from the Bronx and Gambino *consigliere* Frank 'Frankie Loc' LoCascio, set up a porn website to entice users to hand over their credit-card details on a free phone number. Once on the site, the users' back button was disabled and the free phone billed them $59. From there, the porn-site customers received bogus phone calls from the credit company and were rebilled constantly without their permission. In the world of hackers and freakers this concept is known as cramming, as the user gradually gets inundated with numerous porn-site tours. The beauty of these schemes, for the likes of Martino, was that a lot of married men or those in positions of authority were unlikely to go to the police to complain about the frauds. Thousands would deal with the matter privately; only after some considerable effort would they cancel the payments with the co-operation of the banks. The true number of victims of this type of scam is never revealed.

Incredible as it may seem, the illicit porn venture realised an estimated profit of US$300 million for the Gambino coffers, although some put the real figure at double that. It is little wonder that John Gotti realised the potential of men like Martino and LoCascio, as he obviously recognised the power of the new technologies to further the ambition of the Mafia in fresh fields.

Martino and others were later traced by the federal authorities and duly sentenced in 2006 on racketeering charges. As principal organiser, Martino received four years and was fined several million dollars, with his legal fees also in the millions.

Another person in this complex tangled web of porn frauds was businessman Kenneth Matzdorff. He helped Martino set up the communications company to facilitate the frauds but – perhaps revealing the depth, sophistication and longer-term objectives behind this new enterprise – Matzdorff also acquired the Garden City bank in Garden City, Missouri. This would eventually be used to handle everything from credit-card processing to banking customers' money. One can only assume that the idea was that no one would ever be able to cancel their billing arrangements once inside the next wave of frauds – a nightmarish scenario by any standards.

FBI Assistant Director Kevin P Donovan said of the case, 'The charges demonstrate the adaptability of the Gambino crime family. Martino's scheme netted the family hundreds of millions of dollars, befitting his status as the "biggest" earner of all time for the Gambinos.'

Had they managed to continue with the aid of their own merchant bank, the scale of potential frauds to come would be unimaginable, as are the possible proceeds. The era of the Perainos and Dibe certainly pales into insignificance by comparison.

While American law enforcers got to grips with the magnitude of this Gambino-led online fraud, the Russian Mafiya made huge headway in the field. Some experts believe that they are the leading proponents of online pornography and all that entails. A Russian blog site quotes academic Yuri Mamchur as estimating that up to a quarter of the global internet traffic in porn originates from Russian organised crime sources.

A cheap labour force, coupled with a well-educated, computer-literate technorati, have made Russia, Ukraine and some of the Baltic States perfect breeding grounds for porn and cyber-crime. The Russian language is spoken from the Baltic to the Adriatic to the Sea of Japan. It crosses borders into the Islamic world; many people in Turkey are *au fait* with the Russian tongue, as are people on the Asian continent and in much of the former Eastern Bloc. Police corruption, backed up by fearsome ex-KGB staff using military tactics, makes the Mafiya an unstoppable force in this arena.

One recent online con saw thousands of single males duped into parting with money on a bogus Russian brides site. There was a team of phone girls behind the scenes to convince lonely hearts that they were interested in marriage. But these besotted men who had agreed to offers of marriage were, of course, required to provide financial assistance with visas, travel and so on. One German citizen alone lost £26,000 in the marriage swindle. The Swiss-based International Organisation for Migration reckons that the majority of bridal agencies online are now controlled by the Russian Mafiya. A reverse angle on this scam is that the girls in the FSU are recruited into sex slavery with a similar ruse. They are promised rich husbands vetted by an agency (in reality, the Mafiya), but once they travel they find themselves forcibly ensconced in a hellish brothel somewhere without a passport, phone or internet access. One of the key Mafiya lieutenants in the New York prostitution rackets is a Lithuanian woman now sought for questioning by the FBI. The federal authorities homed in on a multimillion-dollar escort agency based in Manhattan called New York Elites, fronted by Elena Trochetchenkova. It seems Trochetchenkova fell foul of the law because her service crossed interstate lines. If a call girl boards a plane to see a client in another state then the offence becomes a federal felony, increasing any potential sentence for the perpetrators.

## PORN AND THE MOB

New York Elites advertised 'European Stunnas' – girls who would perform various sexual activities from coast to coast. Such was the sophistication of the service that hotel rooms were booked in advance and the girls flown around at least 22 states on prearranged tours. Customers were sold the dream that these girls were porn-star escorts. Forget hefty men in suits, this is serious organised crime, generating dream profits. Average prices for the services ranged from US$1,000 to US$2,000 per hour. But most 'stunnas' were shipped in from the FSU, and it is unclear how much they personally saw of the huge profits.

It seems that, although everyone else in the business was arrested, Elena managed to remain at large.

Another favourite pastime of the Russian Mafiya linked with the sex trade is email spamming. Over a billion email users have received some form of Viagra pill advert, penis-enlargement offer or similar spam. These mass email-outs reap large profits for those behind them, who are often on the payroll of pharmaceutical fronts run by organised crime who pay out what is known as an affiliate scheme.

Joe Rosetti, a New York security analyst, stated that Eastern Europe has the most advanced hackers in the world, a concern that has woken up law-enforcement agencies including the Russian Intelligence Service, the FSB. Once perceived as the pastime of nerdy kids pitting themselves against firewalls, some hackers are now aligning themselves with criminal networks. Much of the hacking or fraud work is subcontracted out, often to poor but talented Russian youngsters desperate to earn those elusive riches, while the actual gang members sit back in safety to cream off profits. Moving around different cyber-cafés, the hackers can wreak havoc by raiding bank account details, committing extortion, fraud, deception, spamming and blackmailing those who have surfed porn on their private computers. Considering the degree of the problem, there are few prosecutions to match. Cyber crime is a borderless crime.

The success of the Mafiya, as well as the rapid expansion of their network, is due to their intelligence service-based structure. According to crime experts, the groups are organised in cells similar to those of terrorists and special forces groups. The head of these cells are Pakhans, then there is a brigadier who may have spies watching him to test his loyalty; the various types of operation have street soldiers who do not know who the head of the operation is. It is a loose operation from the outside but inside it is tightly controlled, with draconian penalties meted out to anyone who is disloyal or disobeys the group. Most of the 'Russians' may not in fact be Russian at all, as the former Soviet sphere of influence extends over a wide area of the globe.

One lucrative area for the Russian groups entails porn that is too near to illicit areas to be comfortably filmed in most of the EU, or indeed the US. Here we find barely legal sites, Lolita, drunken teens, hardcore fetishes, involving extreme injury, and now even paedophilia. Russia ranks as the number-two source of paedophilia in the world after the US. All of these sites will be armed with harmful software; everyone knows these days what spyware and Trojan viruses are, but what of keyloggers, diallers, botnets, worms and grayware? Keyloggers will allow the site owners to see what you are typing; grayware is just an annoying feature without much harm to it; diallers will change your internet settings and may clock up a large bill in the process. The revenue from the porn, let alone the crimeware scams, makes John Gotti's enterprise look positively amateurish. A recent calculation taken from media sources gives the worldwide total revenue from porn at US$100 billion, with the Russians said to receive a quarter of this huge sum. It shows the sheer power and wealth behind this industry, much of it in criminal hands. Add the many online scams to this amount and you begin to see why law-enforcement agencies are at a loss to know how to tackle it.

As for the Russian Mafiya, they have numerous resources upon which to call, in terms of money, training, technology and political help, and can find enough hands and guns to rival any police squad. Already the FBI have stated that the Mafiya present a greater threat to national security in the long term than any other group. Interpol has also begun to take the threat seriously after a decade or more of intensive investigation. In January 2008, Semyon Mogilevich, the most senior of all Mafiya figures, was finally arrested. Mogilevich had racked up a US$100 million fortune, much of it allegedly from illicit porn, human trafficking and sex slavery. His other enterprises allegedly included murder, uranium smuggling, extortion and gun running. His arrest signalled a change to the idea of international untouchables – Interpol had irrevocably thrown down the gauntlet to the Mafiya.

### 'Respectable' Business and the Mob

As strait-laced pornographers get rich and successful, at some point in their dealings they are inevitably going to come into contact with organised crime, whether in the form of video piracy, certain software companies, affiliate cash programmes, magazine publishing empires, offshore banks or just investors. Here we must depart from the stereotypical image of burly men in pin-striped suits, fedoras and dark glasses. Dangers are ever present for those who do not know what they are dealing with.

Whenever a British person picks up a copy of the *Express* or the *Star*, do they think of porn? Most would say no. In fact, the newspapers' headlines often condemn porn along with asylum seekers, unemployed people and criminals such as the Mafia. But their proprietor, Richard Desmond, was a pornographer first and foremost, making his fortune through adult publications long before buying his way into the respectable world of newspaper publishing. His first major venture was obtaining the UK rights to *Penthouse* for publication in the UK, which he acquired in the late 1970s from Bob Guccione, the Sicilian-American producer of *Caligula*.

His other steamy publications include *Asian Babes*, *Big Ones*, *Skinny and Wriggly*, *Forum*, *Posh Housewives* and a much vaunted website featuring Anal Annie. Television is also a strong part of his portfolio, including ITVX Europe, Television X and the Fantasy Channel. It has made him immensely wealthy with an estimated fortune of around £600 million.

When Desmond donated money to New Labour, under Tony Blair, a hue and cry went up, as critics viewed it as unseemly to take money from a pornographer, but this may not have been the only reason for their concerns. For Desmond is alleged to have been involved in several murky episodes linked to organised crime.

His company had begun to do business with an American company called Harvest, who would advertise phone sex lines owned by a certain Mr Martino, the gentleman behind the Gambino internet porn scams. But it appears the endeavour went wrong at some stage. One report in *The Independent*, written by Charles Grant, suggested that the argument erupted as Desmond's Northern and Shell attempted to expand in the US. Martino allegedly accused Desmond of fleecing his company of up to a million dollars, advising a friend that Desmond had done this before to others. (Neither accusation is supported, and a Northern and Shell spokesperson claimed that Desmond and Martino had never met.)

The general reports that surfaced alleged Martino warned Desmond that Northern and Shell would be better off staying out of the US altogether. According to these reports, Desmond did not take the threats very seriously at all, and sent an executive called Philip Bailey to set up a business there. Although what happened to Mr Bailey is hotly contested, the FBI released their version of events in a special crime report citing informants close to the scandal. They concluded that Bailey, upon entry into the USA, was allegedly pistol-whipped, threatened, had his face slashed and his testicles tasered by Martino's thugs.

A soldier of the Gambino family is rumoured to have then flown to London to threaten Mr Desmond in person, but the gangster was allegedly rebuffed by the publisher who is said to have called the Mafia man 'stupid' and 'common'. Desmond has consistently dismissed the story as 'pure fantasy'.

A quote from the Meese Commission on organised crime and porn leaves us in no doubt as to how independent vendors will be treated if they do not tow the line with organised crime: 'There was a man who went from New York City ... went into Atlanta. Had films to sell ... They found him at the airport, with a $5,000 Rolex watch on and about eight grand in his pocket, and four rolls of film in his hands, with his head blown up in the trunk of his car. Nobody robbed him, nobody took a dime off him. They didn't even take the film. But he was at the airport with a New York ticket shoved in his coat pocket. Don't come down from New York selling, unless you've been sent down.'

At the same commission, a former FBI agent called Kelly said under oath, 'In my opinion, based upon 23 years of experience in pornography and obscenity investigations and study, it is practically impossible to be in the retail end of the pornography industry without dealing in some fashion with organised crime.'

# Chapter 11

# COMINGS AND GOINGS

## The Schemer

So many of the bizarre characters of the porn world are often misunderstood outlaws or, perhaps more accurately, outsiders. Because of the rapid homogenisation of modern life, it is possible that many will not be around in years to come. Often today, individuals can become so disaffected by the relentless pressure to conform that pornography may serve to represent a very rich vein of human resistance to some. I found myself increasingly compelled to write about them in detail, and I wondered if I was becoming more of a social anthropologist than a writer. However, I settled on the fact that, like them, I wanted nothing to do with certain facets of society.

Let me introduce you to Minton, an Ulsterman who wore as many masks as anyone could; he described himself as an antiques dealer, although he dealt mainly in fakes, but he was also something of an avant-garde pornographer-cum-shambling conman. I would say in his defence that he was a true romantic of our times and a loyal friend to those who knew him, but his penchant for trading under various flags of convenience meant he was well connected in all manner of nefarious business connections – stolen or pirated goods, art forgeries and counterfeit money. Cons of every variety tripped off his tongue as quickly as he could dream them up. He was one of life's mavericks and a very likeable one at that, despite his extremely dishonest streak. Most found him good company, I must say. Sean was his first name – or at least the one he always used in my presence – but he preferred, rather pretentiously in my view, to be known by the nickname Minton after the famous chinaware, seeing himself as something of an expert on Minton pottery as well as other chinaware factories of the 18th and 19th centuries. His Irish skin was china white and contrasted with his shock of jet-black frizzy hair, set against his piercing icy-blue eyes. These eyes made him unnerving at certain interludes, especially when he became animated. He chain-smoked and talked incessantly at all times of the day and night. I never saw him take stimulants, but always suspected that they might be in the background somewhere.

Minton was quite a joker, although the police didn't always see it that way as he had notched up quite a bit of form over the years. There was no love lost between the two of them. Minton hated all police, but hated the antiques squad to the point of obsession.

# COMINGS AND GOINGS

He was a likeable man but definitely something of a fantasist. In terms of his many schemes, think Arthur Daley or Sergeant Bilko; these were the very convoluted plots of an extremely devious mind, but they always seemed to lead nowhere from what I saw or heard about them. Minton had smuggled pirated Armani products that fell apart at the seams before they even got to the market; his turkey heist before Xmas saw the wrong lorry stolen – it was full of pallets; and his foray into the international gemstone trade saw him buying gold chains that were a spray-on job with cheap alloy underneath. Having said that, Minton was never skint.

He was cornered in Italy after the country's TV consumer watchdog exposed a complex art fraud scam, where he was claiming to be a famous artist's grandson who chanced upon a previously unknown art collection. For this little caper he received a prison sentence of one year and nine months.

Minton was indefatigable and, upon his release, as expected by all who knew him, propelled himself with much zest into his latest scheme – the International Bukkake Festival. For those not familiar with the Japanese word Bukkake, it denotes the sexual act of several men ejaculating their semen on to a woman's body or, more typically, face. (Not to be confused with cream pie – the genre showing semen in the vagina.)

Minton had the inspired vision to create a UK-based event where chosen males would ejaculate over models' faces, as big screens displayed it close up to a wider audience who would be inspired to perform a similar feat among themselves. This would be a Bukkake fest in every sense because Minton saw it happening on a grand scale, even going as far as to suggest Olympia or Earl's Court as possible locations.

He pitched his idea to me, as he probably felt I was open-minded enough to listen and knew I understood how to organise events. Of course, I immediately shot down the proposal for health reasons – HIV being a primary concern, not to mention the general legal considerations.

To his credit Minton had made some headway against all the odds, with several hopeful emails from potential sponsors. A Japanese Bukkake producer and a well-known adult award site both showed some interest in the project. His obsessive side seemed to take over with more and more hours being poured into the project, and soon the antiques side of his business became very much a thing of the past. His funds continued to come from areas unknown.

As his financial standing increased, people began to take him more seriously. He purchased a houseboat on the Thames and began to dress more smartly. He morphed from Minton and started calling himself 'the Pearl'. Many who knew him thought this may have been inspired after the slang term for ejaculating over a girl's face – a pearl necklace. Several pretty women emerged from his houseboat – wealth had its own trappings for Minton, who must have been indulging his personal fantasies. He was becoming more eccentric by the day. I suspected drugs were at work here, but Minton loved secretly revelling in his pornographer's status.

## COMINGS AND GOINGS

On one of our final encounters, Minton tried to persuade me to take £3,000 in order to enlist my help with the Bukkake Festival. I remember his skin being very corpse-like and sweaty, a sure sign of drug abuse. But I never forgot the desperate look in his eyes, like something had flown away from his soul. It was like touching a dead man. I flatly refused and left feeling a bit disturbed by the meeting.

Some weeks later, a face-sitting webmaster informed me that Minton wouldn't be around for a while as he had been nabbed in the Caribbean, as part of a multi-million-pound cocaine racket. Apparently, there was a small chance that he could be repatriated to the UK after four years to serve the rest of his sentence in his native country, but only if he pleaded guilty.

Typical of Minton, he fought the case all the way, with a classic cover story. He claimed to the court that his suitcase had been swapped. His own case was full of mangoes or some such cargo. It was a high-risk strategy, bound to fail. I can't say it made any difference to his overall sentence though.

The judge, an expat residing in the Caribbean, is said to have smiled and looked over his half-moon glasses with the words: 'Do you expect this court to believe that there is still a Samsonite suitcase continually revolving on the baggage carousel containing some fruits and your personal belongings?'

The judge gave a restrained titter as the whole court roared with laughter. That merriment soon stopped dead with the announcement of a 12-year prison sentence. Alas, poor Minton, I knew him well. A gentleman and a skullhead.

## The Scheme

Despite his less than successful criminal career, Minton left one internet porn milestone behind him and should be credited with its invention – 'the scheme'. Well, at least I think it originated from him, but of course he may just have crafted and perfected the idea from another source.

This corrupt business model became something of a blueprint for internet fraud in the porn business. The scheme revolves around setting up a site with amateur investors, perhaps people who have a certain fetish or perversion and are desperate to get involved in an organisation or website. Once the website is established – content shot and uploaded, billing system in place and, hopefully, punters paying their subscriptions to look at the private members' area – the sting is in place.

At the crucial moment, everyone involved is informed that the police are investigating an incident, a person, a shipment or whichever story is invented. From there, the respectable people, fearing arrest or investigation, disappear overnight, leaving the schemer with the goods and chattels. He too eventually disappears with everyone's money.

As time went on, other scamsters cottoned on to the scheme. It was developed into progressively more subtle methods of divesting people of their hard-earned cash. The structure of the design formats behind the amateur pay sites around the world are ideal to practise the 'scheme' Minton left as his legacy. Sudden collapsible systems can fold at a moment's notice to leave debtors bereft of their funds. Most recently, the pay-to-view online cinema seemed to be doing this the most. Elsewhere, other forms of the scheme exist.

Minton's idea is the forerunner of the newer, more developed business practices on the net, which incidentally always seem to collapse when the maximum number of clients have joined. The American Mafia are masters of the scheme. Imagine being able to collapse a legitimate bank and walk away with all of the funds. Millions have been lost or gained by this method – depending which side of the fence you are on. Webmasters everywhere will immediately recognise this alarming template.

The scheme has stood the test of time. Many billing systems target webmasters who invest all of their capital in this online banking system. Webmasters are forced to join these credit-processing facilities, as it is the only way they can garner cash from punters who wish to remain anonymous or do not wish to hand over their details to a pornographer. Punters join a site and pay their membership fee to a middleman. It keeps them safe. The nearest approximation is the cheques paid between businesses and their customers. The credit-card processor acts as a secure buffer between the surfer looking for porn and the pornographer. Once the surfer decides he wants to join a site or look at an online cinema, then the credit-card processor takes his details, guaranteeing the legal rights of the buyer, quantifying all purchases of services and then paying the site with the person's money. It is the industry standard in such matters.

But who thought that the middle man would rip anyone off? The Mafia could not resist setting up crooked processing facilities. Thousands of adult webmasters have been ripped off in this way. But there is no one to complain to; after all, the company has collapsed legitimately. My advice to any adult webmaster is to only deal with the Dutch billing companies, no matter what anyone else says.

But Minton left an even greater legacy behind him, although he lost control of it due to his obsession with his Bukkake Festival, and even to this day it is one of the most original ideas in the porn world. I am not aware of any such mass-media event involving sexual activities ever having been broadcast before.

### The Digital Dons

The foundation laid by men like Minton is being increasingly honed and perfected on the internet. There is a new breed of pornographer who has never handled a camera, spoken to a model or probably even bought a top-shelf magazine, yet they are the driving force behind much of the porn being distributed across the net today. These techies are the 'digital dons' – producers of real power. He who controls the technological reins drives the engine of the web. The Mafia, particularly in Russia, have adopted the digital dons' methods and, as often as not, recruited them along with their technical expertise to the ranks of the Mob. The rise of this technorati inside organised crime cannot be overstated.

Firstly, any self-respecting website needs a billing system. Once cash from the punter leaves his bank account for the porn site via a middleman, it can be targeted in a number of ways by the Mafia. But it has to be corrupt in the first place, so reputable website devotees need not overly concern themselves. Then a site needs to market itself to reach a wider audience; the very first marketing tool is the banner link exchange, reciprocal links or banners to share surfers (traffic) with other chosen sites, rather like people who swap business cards with one another. It was a nice idea later corrupted by the digital dons, who developed standalone sites called banner farms. These sites had nothing on them but banner links listed by order of visits per day. But the Mafioso web farm was different. Their banner was always on top of the list even when their traffic ranking was lower than linked sites. Many popular sites were milked of web traffic this way.

Then the straight marketers decided to use TGPs (thumbnail gallery posts), which function like billboards do in towns and cities – in effect, as adverts. The similar-sounding MGPs (movie gallery posts) are identical to TGPs, except they are full of movie files instead of picture galleries.

But this free porn was too much for the advertising boards, and so the businessmen of the web came up with an ingenious idea. They invented the partner program that limited your submissions to one genre and ensured that only relevant people could advertise. So, for example, people with lesbian sites went to lesbian TGPs, Latino sites went to Latino TGPs, and so on. This system worked very well at first, before this too was circumnavigated by the Mafia and some of the bigger studios who flooded the TGP galleries with their content. The bigger studios were by now cottoning on to the need for the digital dons' expertise. It led to a situation where one or two studios dominated a group of TGPs, leaving the little guy out in the cold. This suited people like the Mafia and the very biggest producers, but it began to make porn less versatile. Eventually, democratic submission software like Chameleon was developed, to make submitting to TGPs fairer and stop the spammers and scammers. The balance had been redressed once more.

But ever more crafty ways of ripping people off were developed; as the web producers became more savvy, the Digital Dons turned their attention back to the punters. First came the diallers, which altered the way you connected to the internet and left you with a hefty phone bill, but broadband finished that one off. Then spywares were developed to rinse credit-card details; the latest one is the billing system that rebills your bank even when you have cancelled your porn membership. It is no-nonsense fraud but few complain. There are a myriad of these tricks out there like 'the circle jerk' – a series of blind links that lead nowhere and keep the surfer in the Mafioso hub of sites.

For the latest tips on avoiding these digital cut-purses, there is a wonderful resource called, quite aptly, www.gofuckyourself.com. From here, you can contact adult webmasters who will steer the inexperienced away from the perils of all manner of digital trickery. In the UK, you can attend the irregular meets of www.beerandbollocks.com, also a resource for adult webmasters.

# CHAPTER 12

# THE DENOUEMENT

## Bulgaria

In the civilised precincts of Fitzrovia, London, I attended a meeting of Anglo-American film producers who wanted to finance a series of new sexploitation movies. Think *Lemon Popsicle* with more tits or the mondo films of the early sixties. It was American money and British expertise. My own role would be location manager-cum-consultant, but before opening my mouth I wanted a contract. Talk is cheap: I wanted to see the colour of their money. There were far too many people who touted these ideas, and it was perfectly possible to spend maybe half a year attending meets of this kind. Ever the cynical optimist, I made it abundantly clear that I wanted paying. The Yanks liked that, as they knew I could deliver. The British were

223

a bit taken aback by this sudden brash demand, but I got what I wanted – an advance payment of good faith.

They wanted a prison-camp scenario filmed in one of the former Eastern Bloc countries, to take advantage of cheap film stock, lower rental costs and better tax breaks. Did I know of any former prison camps they could use? I said I had an English-speaking contact in Bulgaria with some influence; they should give me two weeks to research everything and come back to them.

Three weeks later I was in Bulgaria to meet my English contact, who I'll call Damien. His expertise was buying land, chalets and bars in Bulgaria, which he had been doing since the country had opened up to the outside world. Damien had fostered contacts from local villagers and estate agents right through to NGOs, and his prime contact to help this project along was a former close-protection bodyguard.

Early reports suggested that a number of ex-air force bases might become available at a price, and filming would be easy there as long as a few palms were greased. I gave the specs of the films and several locations were suggested. We visited an airfield with hangars, but it soon became apparent that nearby flights would make the sound recording a nightmare. Another location seemed to look good from the outside, but lorries carrying potatoes were a constant threat to both life and limb on the roads that traversed the military base.

Then there was an old abandoned government warehouse that looked grim and foreboding, complete with barbed-wire posts, giving it a concentration-camp feel. It was also cheap.

# THE DENOUEMENT

It seemed Damien had already gone ahead and suggested that a number of local girls be interviewed for parts in the films, and, as he and I surveyed the warehouse fences, an unfortunate tale came via a local messenger about the sad fate of the bodyguard. Now, I have no idea what Damien told the bodyguard to tell people, or if something was lost in translation, but it transpired that the man had been shot dead by angry villagers. It seemed a group of locals believed he was attempting to persuade girls to become involved in prostitution, and what was even more unfortunate was that a lot of the local people knew he was working for us. Damien seemed completely unconcerned by this little fact.

I was aware that this could be a Bulgarian non-computer version of the 'scheme'; after all, we had seen no corpse. But there again, self-preservation was paramount.

I was shocked, and a certain panic was rising within me. 'You mean to say we are talking about creosoting a fence when someone has been shot in the head five times?'

Damien remained seemingly unfazed, but I knew we could not afford to take chances.

'Everyone in the village knows we are all three connected. Everyone here knows we are filmmakers who hired this man. What if they come looking for us?'

Damien seemed detached. 'This sort of shit happens all the time out here.'

I began to wonder if Damien was part of the 'scheme'. Adrenalin was rising, along with anger. 'I want to get out of here now.' I left him alone still inspecting the fence.

As I threw my things into a rucksack, I realised we had a conspicuous hire car. It was almost out of petrol, so it meant a trip near to the village to tank up again. This could prove dangerous. What could we do?

I made a call from our chalet to the film company in London. I explained the situation carefully, and they advised me to go to the local police, although I don't think they grasped the situation out in rural Bulgaria. Try to imagine the Deep South of the USA, combined with family connections, local sheriff, pissed-off villagers with Kalashnikovs and a couple of foreigners accused of trying to enslave their daughters into a life of prostitution.

Suddenly, Damien ran back in looking sheepish. 'Apparently, there has been a slight misunderstanding. They think we're sex slavers.'

'Oh shit! Do we have any translators?'

'No, he's been shot. The other guy is the bar owner who just told me. He won't risk his business to help us.'

'You know the car's on empty, don't you?' I said.

Damien was looking pale and his eyes were wide as he quickly began to realise we were done for.

I paced up and down for a few minutes. Damien asked me to stop as it was making him nervous.

'It could be one of these situations that is so heavy that nothing actually happens,' I said.

We both burst out laughing; it was partly hysterical, partly to relieve the oppressive tension in the air.

# THE DENOUEMENT

Then my brain kicked in – the Prostinetta Alliance. I made a calm, collected call to Soho and spoke with Artaan, my blood brother, who listened carefully.

As my blood brother he vowed his allegiance, promising us a safe passage out of Bulgaria. I put down the phone feeling a lot safer.

Damien threw up his hands. 'How long? Did you ask him when?'

He was clearly beginning to go to pieces again, and it occurred to me that we needed to bail out to another temporary location.

The sound of the phone startled us both. It was Artaan – four hours and we would be out of the village.

Damien ran and packed, and we fled to the safety of nearby woods armed with a few provisions, water and some toilet roll.

At dusk, four hours later on the dot, a car rolled up, parked, and two broad, squat men got out. We approached them waving like long-lost friends. The two Albanian men acknowledged us impassively; it seemed neither spoke much English. The older one could have been no more than 30. He sported ancient scars of cigarette burns down one arm, where he had obviously been tortured, and a thick white scar across his very mean face told you he was no stranger to violence. The younger one had eyes that seemed dead to any compassion whatsoever; his nose was broken and he had subtle facial scars.

He offered us a cigarette and I noticed he was armed to the teeth. Around his belt, there was a handgun and a sheathed knife. Inside the car were two more hand-guns and a semi-automatic weapon. We were now in no doubt that we were getting out of the village safely. Damien and I sat in the back like well-behaved kids, nodding and saying thanks if offered cigarettes, chocolate or coffee from a flask. Somewhat bizarrely, the Albanians played a CD of the Carpenters, but neither Damien nor I would have dreamt of taking the piss out of their musical tastes. Artaan had come through and earned himself any reward I could muster upon my return.

Near to Sofia, Damien handed over most of his Bulgarian lev and said goodbye. I continued nervously into the capital, where I thanked my bodyguards profusely. Here they disappeared as mysteriously as they had arrived. The pair had picked up $400 equivalent in lev and seemed happy enough, if that is the correct way to describe two of the most sombre men I have encountered.

I checked into a hotel and rang London to sort out the abandoned hire car. The young South African temp who answered the phone told me the managers had gone home for the night – apparently, no one really cared about our plight. I took a flight to Athens.

## Get Your Kicks on Route 55?

After the abrupt abandonment of the Bulgarian film, I found myself on Route E55, a European road traversing Southern and Northern Europe, which takes in many major countries along the way.

# THE DENOUEMENT

I was reeling, having come face-to-face with the dark forces of sex and lust, the downside of the sex industry. Then I was sucked headlong into the vortex of the notorious Route 55 – the silk road of modern-day sex slavery and human trafficking. E55, to me, can only mean the highway of Babalon.

This goddess is best described by occultists as a sexual deity, whose funk perfumes her path, as she sails by in a shiny red sports car leaving trails of cocaine dust and champagne bubbles in her wake. She is Atu 11 in the Tarot, sometimes called Lust or Strength in older packs.

At the Southern tip of E55 is Greece, beginning with the seaside resort of Kalamata; located near the ancient city of Pharai mentioned by Homer, it lies SW of Athens. The olive-groved road leads on to Pyrgos, over the water, then to the northern tip of Greece at Igoumenitsa, crossing the Adriatic Sea to Italy at Brindisi. The E55 clings to the eastern coast of Italy until it heads up into the alpine mountains at Tarvisio, one of the ancient Roman trade routes. Upwards into colder climes, now Southern Austria, the road takes in the historic cities of Salzburg and Linz, then passes to the picture-postcard town of Tabor in the Southern Czech Republic, before reaching the capital Prague and exiting at Bohemia. From here on to Dresden in Germany, through Berlin and up into Denmark, the road enters Copenhagen and ends at Helsinger.

The road took in every crash-out, deadbeat, hustler and zombie along the way: Turkish heroin clans, Albanian gunmen and pimps, thieving smackheads heading in and out of the

German hinterlands, Russian Mafiya, a motley crew of potheads doing their Anjuna casualty bit, Bandido biker gangs, an Italian 'businessman', who asked too many questions, Romanian vagabonds travelling together to the land of milk and honey, some very unsavoury British right-wing skinheads and their Eastern European brethren, gaggles of local pickpockets, drug dealers who abound at every major pitstop, double-dealing hoteliers, rinsers and bruisers of every description. For some reason, the Czechs see it as their God-given duty to out-consume every person in the drinking stakes – their alcoholic prowess was an unnatural aberration, obviously genetic.

E55 was a dodgy place for sure. No one gave a shit.

But there was a code along the road and, once you had that familiar dust on you, no one bothered you. Just don't look at maps or street signs or look too touristy. Always carry a trusty blade or knuckleduster on your person and never flash too much cash at the roadside. Simple stuff really, but worth knowing, particularly down south.

On another plane, it is a beautiful highway full of adventure, rich history and cultural treasures, which is why the story of Route 55 is all the more tragic. Porous borders seep a steady supply of sex slaves, clearly demonstrating that humanity is not progressing as we go into the 21st century, but is being dragged back more than a thousand years. The breakdown of Eastern and Southern Europe since the fall of communism, and the economic dream sold by the wealthier member states, is a poisoned chalice, giving rise to vicious, nomadic gangsters and an endless supply of victims. Murder, rape and fear are on the rise. Anyone who has any doubt should see Route 55 for themselves. Law-enforcement agencies are at a loss, once again resorting to repressive moral penalties as the answer. Politicians, vulnerable to the economic benefits of the sudden influx of cheap labour, may try to fudge the issue. Budapest is now considered the Bangkok of the West, and certainly a porn capital to rival Holland. If you imagine a huge syringe sucking the life blood out of Europe, the forefinger covering the 'Dam, the middle finger poised over Hamburg, the thumb pulling back the ring of the syringe at London, then imagine the flotsam and jetsam of Route 55 being drawn forth by the riches of three principal cities – this is one feeling of the place. It is truly a sad, desolate prospect in that respect, sucking up an ever larger number of 'Natashas' each year.

The Natashas – a term coined by Canadian author Victor Malarek, who wrote a book of the same name – is used to describe the girls in the new international sex-slave trade. It was on Route 55 that I realised why the Bulgarian villagers reacted as they did. Malarek's book tells of an Eastern European girl tempted, or forced, into the sex trade, who experiences all manner of degradation as a result. Few would argue the fact that E55 is associated with the influx of modern slaves. Several border towns at various points have become open-air bordellos offering lines of girls, whose often violent pimps parade them like cattle in the streets. Some have blamed the fall of the Iron Curtain for this trend and dubbed the highway the Iron

Suspender Belt, but it is no joking matter for the police and politicians desperate to stop the vile trade in slave-women. Germany saw a doubling in sex traffic in just three years and has become a major destination for the delivery of cheap prostitutes on to the market. Once liberal towns and cities such as Hamburg are now reconsidering their attitudes towards the sex trade. Poland, then the Czech Republic, are the drop-off points for these unfortunate women taken from the former Soviet states. Then on to the E55. To understand the scale of the trade, consider that just one Polish criminal managed to sell on over 200 women before his arrest. Now think of organised gangs from Russia, Ukraine, Poland, the former Yugoslavia, but particularly Albania, all trading in women, and you begin to comprehend the magnitude of the problem. Interpol, the United Nations and European governments have all started to fight back, but their efforts cannot stem the frightening tide of modern sex slavery, mainly due to its ease and the huge multi-billion-dollar profits. The underbelly of the Adriatic is both the perfect breeding ground and geographical route for sex slavery, where much of the region is in economic and political turmoil, and where corruption and lawlessness flourishes.

## The Champagne Bubble Bursts

Back in London after my road trip, I felt little better. I had long resigned as location manager. The film company had not behaved responsibly, and it was clear that we were just expendables.

# THE DENOUEMENT

Wandering around Soho, I suffered a series of further shocks as I bumped into Lexie, the pretty, petite blonde I had once dated in Brighton. She had grown plump, cellulite folded skin hung grotesquely over her waistline, exposed by her crop top. Her features were bloated, with lines under her eyes. What had happened in so short a time? Over coffee she told me she was working as a champagne hostess by night. Clients would drink champagne with the girls, who got paid by how many glasses the client ordered. Naturally, the girls consumed as much of the lovely bubbly as they could. To drink this much booze, one imagined that cocaine would be needed to keep the hostess girls straight enough to talk. Lexie confirmed that she was in the throes of taking the drug night after night, and drinking loads. Formerly, she had been teetotal and a non-user. The results of excess on her tiny frame were shocking to me. It was clear evidence that she was killing herself. She seemed burned out, but still very pretty beneath the tiredness. She told me that it was not out of the question for her to earn over a thousand pounds on a good couple of nights, and she had wisely saved most of the money for driving lessons and an MA in fine art. Her dream was to become an interior designer. I urged her to leave the champagne lifestyle immediately, as she looked terrible. I truly believe that it is one industry the government should look at as a matter of urgency; I think that, in the future, it will be looked back on almost as people nowadays view children working in factories or as chimney sweeps, as pure, dangerous exploitation.

But, as ever, it wasn't all doom and gloom with Lexie. She told me one very funny story that made me laugh, as she always had done in the past. It centred on a sex party in south London, organised by two new rather greedy interlopers who sought to make a quick buck. The two wide boys hailed from Essex and were, to say the least, a mercenary pair, not even genuine perverts with a background in the sex industry. They believed that all they needed to do was hire some 'tarts', to use their phrase, get hold of a discreet venue and advertise. All the elements came together and they ended up with one English girl, two Czechs and a manageress-cum-entertainer. Twenty-odd mug punters turned up at the new party and it began with a bang. Everything was good until some bright spark – Lexie suspected it was the two wide boys themselves – put super-Viagra in some of the drinks. It could have been mixed with a drug called GHB, or ecstasy. The result was a surge of rampant old men with hard-ons from hell. The Czech girls went on strike after about an hour of non-stop pounding. The clients were beside themselves, possibly under the influence of whatever it was in the drinks. In their sexual frustration, they turned on the organisers, who were trapped in the corner of a room by some 15 to 20 naked old men sporting erections, all of whom were pressing forwards, angrily demanding their money back. The details of what happened next are not clear, but we are left in no doubt that the Essex boys certainly came up against a rock and a hard place, to quote the good book.

And, on an even happier note, I have heard since then that Lexie has quit the champagne hostess business, slimmed down again and moved to Dubai to work for a design company. She is now engaged to an Arabian businessman.

I arrived home after the meeting with Lexie to some bad news: Steve the Spank had reared his ugly head once more. Firstly, it seemed he was badmouthing other influential producers online, starting rumours and questioning provenance. Secondly, he had started a war over control of an escort business. I began to realise that the rumours we had heard, that several people had already tried to kill Steve in the past, may well have been true. But, like a cat with nine lives, he had always escaped unscathed.

Naturally, the existing website owner had no intention of losing control and enlisted the help of the escorts, who demanded that their names be removed from all of Steve's sponsored prostitution sites; as a result, Steve lost control of a vast amount of web traffic. Sniffing dollars and seeing that Steve was down on his luck, the website owner pressed home his advantage and moved in for the kill, acting as sponsor to replace Steve in many places on the net. He then managed to get Steve blacklisted, including on one of his billing systems.

An anonymous source started issuing death threats once more, but this time they were more pressing, as Steve's latest address in Manchester had come to light and spread like wildfire on the net. He had no choice but to bring in the police for his own protection. The police decided to contact his 'wife' with regards to the death threats, but it seems hell hath no fury like a woman scorned. Within days, Steve's wife called film distributors and took control of the copyright of all of his back catalogue. The financial damage from this and the website owner's actions were catastrophic.

Apparently, Steve continues to run a small hub of sites very discreetly south of Manchester, but by all accounts is a broken man. It seems that no one cares, however, demonstrating clearly that life is about giving, not taking.

## The Square Root of Tomorrow

If I had not had enough shocks to last a lifetime, there was a double A-side release with further tremors to come. News broke that Artaan had been badly wounded in Albania. There were few details of how, why and where. I noticed that the Albanians I had known in Soho were thinning out, either jailed, bailed, moved on or gone back home. Those remaining were unfriendly, not wanting to talk.

To say I was reeling was an understatement. So much had happened in a few days.

Lots of job offers were coming in but I was numbed to them.

One of them was made by a Russian-sponsored businessman I didn't even know. His brash offer was definitely at the wrong time, wrong place.

'Look inside the bag.'

I opened the bag and marvelled as it was full of neatly bundled notes, mostly stacks of twenties but some fifties. '£52K. It's yours if you wanna walk out with it here and now. That's 52 films over a year or so. Take it and we shake on 52 films.' Dmitri shifted into the back of his chair and, with a benign smile, crossed his hands in a priestly gesture.

'But you don't even know me. I don't know what type of films you want.' I was shocked.

'I want product and, believe me, if I wanted to know you I could; besides, you come highly recommended from a very good friend of mine.'

It was relaxed but I wasn't taking the bait. North London is a dangerous place for a guy to walk around with £52K. After some thought, Dmitri tossed two bundles of money extracted from a drawer in his desk, shifting forward and dragging the bag back towards him to replace it by his side.

'You work for me, OK? A lot of people say you can shift anything. Are you in the firm?'

I thought he was joking. He was the only one in the firm – a Russian one.

This was one of many organised crime offers that I walked away from. It was tempting, because that initial investment of £52k could potentially have been turned into £520K in less than a year, depending on shooting schedules. My own cut would have been 15–20 per cent.

Another more benevolent landlord in Soho offered me a gentleman's club, a members' champagne bar, not the sort Lexie worked in but a respectable lap-dancing club. It was to be billed 'the Reverends' or something equally sacrilegious. The only thing was that the backers were oriental, from the wrong side of Shaftesbury Avenue. I could foresee trouble and declined, although once again the spoils would have made life very comfortable, no doubt. Or I could have been the richest man in the graveyard.

Thanks to the trip I made to Amsterdam, offers were coming in thick and fast, as if to mock my state of nervous exhaustion. I had finally made the field of dreams as far as commercial recognition was concerned. I was put in touch with award-winning model Jasmine St Clair and variously offered editorship of *Roue* magazine (the Rolls-Royce of British spanking), management of another champagne establishment in another part of London and control of an escort business in E1, with a man known as the Maitre D' (so called because he could always serve whatever the kinky clients wanted). Another offer was for me to act as conduit of Latino distribution between Brazil and London – it seemed the list of offers was endless. But I needed a rest – I was physically fatigued as well as emotionally drained.

After all, I had seen spanking parties; filmed a dominatrix urinating into the mouth of a devotee until his mouth was full and overflowing, before he was ordered to swallow the liquid in one; witnessed at first hand people tied to crosses and molested by groups of desperate, sex-starved men; heard young twinks barely out of college talking about the art of figging, where roots of ginger were put inside their anus (as practised by the Victorians) before they were birched; seen group 'rapes' conducted by women on clearly disturbed men who could not get off any other way; spied from a sordid peephole on customers playing marbles with a girl paid to dress in school uniform, where no sex was involved; smelled the cloying PVC and rubber of slaves at close hand as they begged to go the Queening Throne and be face-sat; partied hard with one particular model, the only girl I know who can polish off a bottle of vodka in 45 minutes, load up with a mountain of special K and still walk away sober' I could on. This is not to mention what I have seen on film, from genital electrodes to dogging, both amateur and professional.

My mind had reached its saturation point. I needed a well-earned break from this world for a while.

# EPILOGUE

Back in the one-time bondage dungeon in Brighton, the room took on a sympathetic countenance, if that can be said of a room. It was always a strange place and, if a room could have emotions, then this one seemed to understand me. Time itself seemed to stand still within it and this was borne out by one or two visitors' observations, not prompted by me. The journey was over, the room appeared to be saying. Members of the occult-inspired ritual performance band, HRT, visited the bondage dungeon and one member of the band even slept in it for several weeks. But the room began to change, as if resentful that I was going back into that world, almost like a jealous lover. It seems mad to write this now, but that is how powerful an environment the bondage dungeon was. I felt her talons on my back several times.

She unnerved me so much that I decided to leave. It was obvious she no longer wanted me as I was, and, to be honest, I no longer needed her as I once did. The book was finished and so was our relationship. Before I left, the flat caught alight, destroying many of my belongings, and the so-called salvage team did the rest. Their handiwork left me without 11 years of my writings, photos of dead friends and precious mementos. I blame the vindictive nature of the bondage dungeon as much as anything. She had her lunar periods, like any woman.

The very last time I left the fire-damaged property, I realised that I had a bad chest, my eyesight was fuzzy and I was going down with something. I had a dose of really bad flu that laid me out for three days. I have never been so ill, except for contracting scarlet fever in my youth.

The bondage dungeon was both the beginning and the end of the tale. It left me completely without possessions – most fakirs and mystics of the East spend decades trying to attain this state, but here I was. Within days I accepted the loss and realised that, though it is completely true that we are very attached to material items, they mean nothing when it comes to it. I was ill, and low, but when that passed I was, to a degree, reborn. It didn't mean that troubles had left me by any means, but I had been given a chance to see what is important about life. Material things are worthless compared with people, your senses, nature, enjoyable food and pastimes, friendship, laughter, love and sex. In my newfound elevated state, I found it hard to go backwards; many people I had known before seemed so cardboard and two-dimensional, they were too easy to read. I got on a train and left Brighton to start a new life.

Hopping off a train at Farringdon, I came across the Maitre D', who had resumed a musical career; it was Christmastime and we had a pint at Clerkenwell Green.

As we left the boozer we joined a group of Christians singing Christmas carols. It was really uplifting, joyous and totally innocent. Festive cheer descended on us both.

After a few carols we decided to move on. A young woman handed us a church leaflet as we began to walk away, but the Maitre D' said, 'It's OK, he's a reverend. We don't need one.'

'Which denomination are you?' she said suspiciously.

'Porn-again Christian,' came my quick answer.

She must have misheard me as she said, beaming, 'You are very welcome to join us again, Reverend.'

I took the leaflet, while the Maitre D' noted she was quite fit.

The bondage dungeon in Brighton may be, to my mind, comparable to the churches of Hawksmoor, unusual places where dark energies are said to amass and strange events unfurl, eddy and resonate around their portals. I am sure Hawksmoor knew, like his mentor Sir Christopher Wren, that the churches must be built on ancient Pagan sites, or some such place of power, in order to fulfil their service. The tiny bondage dungeon was no exception.

More than 15 people that I was first in contact with while writing this book have died or gone missing. Several are now facially disfigured as a result of working in the porn industry – and that is just from organised crime, let alone bad plastic surgeons. Some, like Tony, Martina and Lexie are happy and contented, having taken exactly the right measure to be successful and then retired with the cash.

I was one of the lucky ones, as I had the bondage dungeon that allowed me to measure myself against the forces around me at any given moment, and I never lost sight of that. Babalon (the Great Whore) was with me at all times.

My phone has recently been ringing, telling me of the coming recession in the porn world; models with no work; webmasters no longer getting their rocks off; the casting couch lying cold and dry from disuse; even pimps are complaining about the lack of custom, blaming their woes on the so-called credit crunch. But I have to keep my perspective far from money and market forces.

If you want my personal opinion, I have stepped over a thick red line, the lipstick of Babalon; I have seen a place where anything was possible, where everyday was colourful, dangerous, beautiful, creative, invigorating and sometimes cruel but always real. Here self-discovery lay before me at any given moment. But, sadly, the punters have only glimpsed what they paid for before the shutters went down on their 'What the Butler Saw' reality, before returning safely home.

Now I am the Reverend once more; I walk along any number of

## EPILOGUE

British streets and see people who like to think their teenage kids are not having unprotected sex. Talk to them and they'll tell you they don't surf porn – never have done. But the porn industry accounts for a third of internet surfers as its audience; its revenues are billions of pounds each year; someone is buying it, and it's not the youngsters.

I may have crossed back into the grey world of respectability but I see it as a world of hypocrites, self-denial, repression, almost schizoid separation between libido and social conditioning. I am glad I discarded that old baggage years ago. I am the last one who needs to buy top-shelf magazines, visit a bondage dungeon, lust after an organised orgy or surf porn on the net … it's a busman's holiday, mate. I can truly say I am beyond it all.

I hear Babalon's intoxicated laughter taunting my senses. Soon it will pass.